Freelancer & Independent Contractor Expense Tracker:

A Concise Self-Employment Tax Record Book to Track Income, Expenses, and Tax Set-Asides (Schedule C)

By A. Herrick

By A. Herrick

Freelancer & Independent Contractor Expense Tracker: A Concise Self-Employment Tax Record Book to Track Income, Expenses, and Tax Set-Asides (Schedule C)

First edition
Christiansted, US Virgin Islands: A. Herrick, 2026

230 pages, 8.5 by 11 inches

Business | Accounting Records and Bookkeeping | Sole Proprietors | Schedule C Filers

ISBN 978-1-960427-58-8

Library of Congress Control Number: Not assigned

657.2

A. Herrick's books may be purchased in bulk for premiums, groups, educational, business or sales promotional use. For information, please write to: Amy@AmyRoseHerrick.com.

Disclaimer: The information and/or documents contained in this book do not constitute legal or financial advice and should never be used without first consulting with other professionals to determine what may be best for your individual needs. The publisher and the author do not make any guarantee or other promise as to any results that may be obtained from using the content of this book. The publisher and the author make no guarantees concerning the level of success you may experience by following the advice and strategies contained in this book, and you accept the risk that results will differ for everyone. Although the publisher and the author have made every effort to ensure that the information in this book was correct at press time, and while this publication is designed to provide accurate information in regard to the subject matter covered, the publisher and the author assume no responsibility for errors, inaccuracies, omissions, or any other inconsistencies herein and hereby disclaim any liability to any party for any loss, damage, or disruption caused by errors or omissions, whether such errors or omissions result from negligence, accident, or any other cause. If any names are used in any illustration, they have been changed to protect the privacy of the individual.

This Book Belongs To

Name: ______________________________

Business Name: ______________________________

Tax Year: ______________________________

Contact Info: ______________________________

____

Content

Introduction

If you're a freelancer or independent contractor, you already know the truth: you don't just do the work. You do the work and the paperwork and the "Wait... where did that receipt go?" scavenger hunt.

This book is here to end the scavenger hunt.

You bought this because you want clean, simple records that make tax season easier—and (even better) help you run your work like a real business, whether you're a consultant, designer, writer, handyperson, therapist, photographer, tradesperson, coach, gig worker, or any other 1099-style independent worker.

What this book does (and what it doesn't)

This is a recordkeeping tool. It's designed to help you track income, expenses, invoices, payments, job costs, travel, and the "messy middle" stuff that often gets forgotten until year-end.

This is not tax advice, and it's not a tax form. It's a practical system so you can hand your tax pro clean information—and so you can see your own numbers clearly while you're earning them.

Why freelancers get burned (and how this fixes it)

Freelancers usually don't get in trouble because they're doing anything shady. They get in trouble because the work comes first, and the tracking gets postponed... and postponed... and then suddenly it's March and your bank deposits don't match your invoices and you're trying to remember what that $186 charge was from last July.

This tracker solves the three biggest freelancer problems:

1. "I made money, but I don't know what I actually kept."
   Use the job/project pages to track what you earned, what it cost you to deliver, and what the project was truly worth.

2. "Clients are slow-paying, and I lose track of what's owed."
   Use the invoice + collections pages (and the A/R aging view you're adding) so you're not guessing.

3. "My deposits don't match my invoices."
   Payment processors, fees, partial payments, refunds, and chargebacks make your bank feed look like a crime scene. There's a section that helps you reconcile deposits, so your records reflect reality.

How to use this book without overthinking it

You do not need a perfect system. You need a consistent one.

- **Set up once: Pick the pages that match your work.**
- **Track weekly: Ten minutes a week beats ten hours in April.**
- **Do a monthly mini-close: Reconcile payment processor deposits, check invoices still owed, and file receipts.**

OPTIONAL pages (so this still fits every freelancer)

Not every freelancer runs paid ads. Not every freelancer receives non-cash products. Not every freelancer sells physical inventory. That's why several sections are (and should be clearly labeled) OPTIONAL—use only if it applies to your work.

If a page doesn't apply, skip it with confidence. This book is meant to fit *your* business, not force you into someone else's.

Now it I time to turn the page. Let's make "future you" grateful.

Who This Book Is For / Who It Is Not For

This book is for you if...

You're a freelancer or independent contractor who wants a simple, consistent system to track income and expenses without turning your life into an accounting project.

This book is for you if you:

- **get paid by clients for services, projects, retainers, or contract work**
- **invoice clients (or should) and want a clean way to track what's paid vs. still owed**
- **receive payments through ACH, check, Zelle, PayPal, Stripe, Square, or other processors**
- **want your deposits to make sense at year-end (gross paid → fees/refunds → net deposits)**
- **have business expenses that include real-life mixed-use items (phone, internet, vehicle, home office)**
- **hire occasional help (a VA, designer, bookkeeper, subcontractor) and want year-end to be clean**
- **want to hand your tax professional organized records instead of a pile of mystery charges**
- **want fewer surprises at tax time—especially around quarterly set-asides and 1099 forms**

If your income is uneven month to month, that's normal. This book was built for that.

This book is not for you if...

This book is not the right fit if:

- **You are a W-2 employee only and your employer withholds taxes from your paycheck**
- **You want a book that teaches you tax law step-by-step or replaces professional advice**
- **You run a business with employees and want to track payroll here (payroll needs payroll software/service)**

- **You operate a full retail business with large inventory, multiple locations, or complex sales tax compliance**
  (This book includes optional pages for COGS/sales tax, but it's not a full retail system.)
- **You want automated tracking or software integration (this is a practical workbook, not an app)**
- **You plan to "catch up later" and don't intend to use any tracking system consistently**

If you're somewhere in the middle...

A lot of independent workers are hybrid:

- **mostly services, with an occasional product sale**
- **mostly domestic clients, with a few international payments**
- **mostly direct payments, with some processor payments and fees**

That's fine. This edition includes optional pages for those situations—use what applies and skip the rest.

Bottom line: If you're self-employed and need a clean, realistic way to track what you earn, what you spend, and what you keep—this book is for you.

IMPORTANT NOTE (PLEASE READ)

This book is a recordkeeping tool — not legal, tax, or financial advice.

This workbook was created to help freelancers and independent contractors stay organized, track income and expenses consistently, and keep clean records that support self-employed tax reporting (including Schedule C where applicable). It is not a substitute for professional tax, legal, or payroll advice.

Tax rules can be technical, and they change over time. Requirements related to areas such as:

- **1099 reporting**
- **sales tax (when applicable)**
- **international payments**
- **mixed-use expenses**
- **travel deductions**
- **payment processor reporting and deposit reconciliation**
  may shift from year to year due to updates in tax law, regulations, or IRS guidance.

To keep this book useful and evergreen:

- **Rules and thresholds can change. Always confirm current-year requirements.**
- **Examples in this book are educational. They demonstrate practical recordkeeping methods, not final tax determinations.**
- **When in doubt, verify with a qualified professional. Your tax professional can apply current rules correctly to your specific situation.**

Used properly, this workbook helps reduce errors, improve compliance, and save time—because good records make good decisions possible.

FOR YOUR TAX PROFESSIONAL

This workbook is designed to support accurate, well-organized recordkeeping for freelancers and independent contractors, including those who report self-employed income (Schedule C where applicable).

Expenses, worksheets, and summaries are grouped by common reporting categories and kept separate where clarity matters—especially in common freelancer "risk zones" such as:

- **payment processor and banking fees (why deposits don't match invoices)**
- **refunds, adjustments, and chargebacks (when applicable)**
- **invoice and payment tracking (paid vs. still owed)**
- **client project costs and reimbursables (job-related profitability and clean substantiation)**
- **mixed-use items (phone, internet, vehicle, home office)**
- **equipment/asset tracking and major purchases to review (for proper classification)**
- **international client payments and currency conversion notes (when applicable)**
- **cost of goods sold and sales tax tracking (only if the taxpayer sells physical products)**

When used consistently throughout the year, this format is intended to reduce reclassification, follow-up questions, and year-end reconstruction—so you can focus on proper application of current tax law instead of recreating records or chasing missing details.

In short: this workbook is built to provide a cleaner package—more complete, more consistent, and easier to verify.

How to Use This Book

This book is your paper trail: a simple, practical system to track business income and expenses all year so tax time is boring (in the best way).

If you're a freelancer or independent contractor, the real problem usually isn't "doing taxes."

It's finding what you spent, proving what you spent, and remembering *why* you spent it—months later—when your memory is conveniently on vacation.

This tracker fixes that.

What This Book Does (and Doesn't Do)

This book helps you:

- Track business income and expenses in a clean, consistent way
- Organize common freelancer/independent contractor deductions
- Keep quick notes that make expenses defensible (audit-resistant)
- Total your numbers so you (or your tax pro) can prepare self-employment reporting faster (Schedule C where applicable)
- Reduce "surprise tax bills" by helping you see patterns and plan ahead

This book does NOT:

- Replace a tax professional (or IRS instructions)
- Automatically categorize expenses for you (sorry—this isn't magic)
- Track W-2 wages or payroll (if you have employees, use payroll software/service)

Quick disclaimer: This book supports organization and education—not individualized tax advice. Rules change. If you are in doubt, ask your tax professional.

Before You Start (10 Minutes That Save You Hours Later)

Step 1: Choose your tracking method

Pick one approach and stick to it:

- **By date (most common and easiest)**
- **By project/client (best if you want to see profitability by job)**

Step 2: Decide how you'll separate business from personal

If you do nothing else, do this:

- **Use a separate business account or card, or**
- **Commit to marking business transactions clearly and consistently**

Because your bank app is not a bookkeeping system. It's just a list of... choices.

Step 3: Set your "receipt system"

Choose one:

- **Envelope/folder for paper + one monthly scan day**
- **Digital folder by month (Jan, Feb, Mar...)**
- **Receipt app (fine—but still reconcile monthly)**

Weekly Routine (5–10 Minutes)

Your goal is consistency—not perfection.

Each week:

1. **Record income received (payments, deposits, retainers).**
2. **Record expenses paid.**
3. **Add a short note when needed:**
    - **What was it for?**
    - **What was the business purpose?**
    - **Was any personal portion included?**

Examples of "good notes" (simple, not dramatic):

- **"Adobe subscription — client deliverables"**
- **"Parking — client meeting"**

- "Printer ink — invoices + client packets"
- "Laptop stand — home office equipment"

If someone ever asks, "What was this for?" your notes should answer without you needing a séance.

Use Categories the Way the IRS Thinks

This book is designed to support self-employed tracking (Schedule C style, where applicable). Common freelancer/independent contractor categories include:

- Advertising & marketing (website, ads, business cards, networking)
- Software & subscriptions (cloud storage, invoicing, project tools)
- Supplies (paper, ink, small office items, job materials)
- Equipment (computer, printer, specialized tools—may need special handling)
- Phone & internet (business portion)
- Professional services (legal, accounting, bookkeeping, tax prep)
- Contract labor (subcontractors/outsourced help—W-9/1099 considerations)
- Travel & mileage (client travel, parking, tolls)
- Meals (only when legitimate business rules are met)
- Banking/processing fees (when payments are reduced by fees)

Important: Some expenses are mixed-use (phone, internet, vehicle, home office). Track a reasonable business-use percentage consistently and keep a short note.

Income Tracking (Don't Skip This)

Freelancers under-track income because:

- payments arrive from multiple clients and methods
- processing fees reduce deposits
- deposits get batched or delayed
- a 1099 may not match what hit the bank

Track income from:

- client payments (ACH, check, Zelle, wire, etc.)
- payment processors (Stripe/PayPal/Square, etc.)
- retainers and deposits
- reimbursables (if you bill them)

Best practice: Track what you received (and what was withheld as fees), so the math is explainable.

Monthly Closeout (20–30 Minutes)

Once a month, do a mini closeout:

1. Compare your entries to bank/credit card statements
2. Make sure anything business-related is captured
3. Add notes to anything unclear while you still remember
4. Confirm your totals (or complete monthly totals if your pages include them)

This is the difference between:

- "Tax time took 2 hours," and
- "Tax time took 2 weeks and a small emotional breakdown."

Quarterly Routine (Because Freelancers Don't Have Withholding)

At the end of each quarter:

- Review income and expenses
- Look at your net profit trend
- Set aside funds for estimated taxes (your tax pro can help you estimate)

Rule of thumb (not a guarantee): if you don't set aside something, tax season will set it aside for you—painfully.

Tax-Time Hand-Off (Make This Easy on Yourself)

When it's time to file, this book helps you deliver clean information fast. Provide totals (and receipts when needed) for:

- income totals
- expenses by category
- mileage totals (if applicable)
- large equipment purchases
- home office info (if you qualify)
  Also gather:
- any 1099s you received
- W-9/W-8 forms for contractors you paid (if applicable)

If You're Hiring Help (Important)

If you pay people who are not your employees (subcontractors, VAs, designers, bookkeepers, project support), you typically need:

- the right tax form on file (often W-9 for U.S. contractors)
- clean payment records
- possible year-end reporting requirements

This book helps you track what you paid. It does not file 1099s for you.

The "Do This Even If You're Busy" List

If you're slammed and can only do the basics:

1. Track income weekly
2. Track expenses weekly
3. Reconcile monthly to your bank/credit card statements

That's it. That's the system.

Final Note (from someone who has seen the mess)

The IRS doesn't require perfection.
But they do require records.

This tracker helps you build records that make sense, hold up, and keep your financial life from turning into a shoebox of panic.

QUICK START: YOU CAN START USING THIS BOOK IN 15 MINUTES

You can start using this book in 15 minutes. The goal is not perfection. The goal is consistent, defensible records that make tax time easy.

Step 1 — Write These 5 Things First (2 minutes)

Fill out the "Owner / Business Info" page (or write this on the first page if you don't have one):

- **Your name (and business name, if any)**
- **Tax year: ________**
- **Business type: Freelancer / Independent Contractor**
- **Primary income sources (check all that apply):**
  ☐ Client services (project or hourly)
  ☐ Retainers / deposits
  ☐ Reimbursables billed to clients
  ☐ Other: ______________________
- **Primary payment methods you use:**
  ☐ Business bank account
  ☐ Personal bank account (temporary)
  ☐ Business credit card
  ☐ Check / ACH / wire / Zelle
  ☐ PayPal / Stripe / Square / other processor: _______________

Step 2 — Pick Your Tracking Rhythm (1 minute)

Choose one and commit:

☐ **Weekly (best for most freelancers)**
☐ **Daily (only if your volume is high)**
☐ **Twice a month**
☐ **Monthly (only if your volume is low and you're disciplined)**

If you wait until tax season, your memory will lie to you. That's just science.

Step 3 — Choose Your Receipt System (2 minutes)

Pick the easiest option you'll actually do:

☐ Digital by month (Jan–Dec folders)
☐ One paper envelope per month + one monthly scan day
☐ Receipt app + monthly export/download
☐ "Inbox folder" + weekly sort (good enough if consistent)

Rule: If you can't support it, it can become a problem when it counts.

Step 4 — Start With Income (5 minutes)

Freelancers lose money at tax time when income is messy.

Use the income pages to track gross income received, including:

- **client payments (project fees or hourly work)**
- **retainers / deposits**
- **reimbursables collected (if applicable)**

Important: If you get paid through PayPal/Stripe/Square, track the fees as expenses—not as "missing income."
That keeps your numbers clean and explainable.

Step 5 — Track Expenses Using the "Business Purpose" Rule (5 minutes)

Every expense should pass this simple test:

Would I still buy this if I didn't have the business?

- **If yes, it may be personal or mixed-use. Track only the business portion and add a note.**
- **If no, it's likely a business expense.**

For each expense entry, record:

- **Date**
- **Vendor**

- Amount
- Category
- Business purpose note (one short phrase)

Examples of simple, audit-proof notes:

- "Software subscription — client project work"
- "Parking — client meeting"
- "Domain renewal — business website"
- "Printer ink — invoices + client packets"
- "Subcontractor help — Project X support"

The "Do This Every Week" Routine (10 minutes)

Once a week, do this quick reset:

1. Enter income received this week
2. Enter expenses paid this week
3. File receipts (or drop them into your monthly folder)
4. Add notes to anything that won't make sense later
5. Mark the week complete (or total it if your pages allow)

Monthly Closeout (20–30 minutes)

At the end of each month:

- Compare entries to bank/credit card statements
- Catch missing expenses
- Reconcile deposits (especially if you use processors)
- Total the month (or complete the totals page)

This one habit saves hours and prevents year-end "mystery deposit" problems.

Two Freelancer Mistakes This Book Helps You Avoid

1. **Mixing business and personal spending with no notes (the fastest way to lose deductions)**
2. **Ignoring fees (processor/banking fees add up—track them)**

If You Only Use 3 Sections, Use These

If time is tight, focus on:

1. **Income tracking**
2. **Expense tracking**
3. **Monthly totals / summary**

That alone is enough to make tax prep faster and cleaner.

Final Reminder

This book supports self-employed recordkeeping (Schedule C style, where applicable). It won't file your taxes—but it will keep you from paying extra taxes just because your records were a mess.

THE FREELANCER AND INDEENDENT CONTRACTOR MONEY MAP

(A simple system to keep your money organized, your taxes funded, and your business predictable—even when your income isn't.)

If you're a freelancer, contractor, or gig worker, your money has a special talent: it shows up in bursts... and disappears in silence.

This "Money Map" gives every dollar a job the moment it arrives—so you're not guessing at tax time, scrambling at bill time, or pretending you'll "catch up later" (famous last words).

The Core Rule

All income hits one landing spot first.
Then you split it into buckets on purpose.

Because if you don't assign the money a job, it will happily assign itself one. Usually something with a "Buy Now" button.

The Money Map Flow

Money IN → Split → Spend/Save/Pay Taxes → Pay Yourself

Step 1 — Choose Your Money Map Level

Pick the version you'll actually use.

Option A: The "Keep It Simple" 3-Bucket Map

Best for new freelancers and anyone who hates bookkeeping.

1. **TAX BUCKET (set-aside)**
2. **BUSINESS BUCKET (operating expenses)**
3. **YOU BUCKET (owner pay / personal)**

That's enough to change your life.

Option B: The "Clean & Powerful" 5-Bucket Map

Best if you want control and smoother cash flow.

1. **INCOME LANDING (all deposits go here)**
2. **TAX SET-ASIDE (estimated taxes live here)**

3. **OPERATING EXPENSES (subscriptions, supplies, ad spending, contractors)**
4. **OWNER PAY (your consistent "paycheck")**
5. **PROFIT / RESERVE (buffer + future goals)**

You can do this with separate bank accounts, or with one account + labeled "buckets" if your bank supports it.

Step 2 — Pick Your Split Percentages (Starter Numbers)

These are starting points, not commandments. Your real numbers depend on your income level, deductions, state taxes, and how expensive your business is to run.

Starter split (common for many freelancers):

- **25%–35% → Tax Set-Aside**
- **30%–55% → Operating Expenses**
- **10%–20% → Profit/Reserve**
- **Remainder → Owner Pay**

If you're early stage and your business costs are low, your operating % may be lower and your owner pay higher.
If you have heavy ad spend, contractors, or equipment needs, operating % may be higher.

Important: This book helps you build clean records—not give personalized tax advice. When in doubt, confirm your tax set-aside % with your tax pro.

Step 3 — Run the Money Map (The Weekly Routine)

Pick a day of the week. Same day every week.

Weekly Money Map Checklist (10 minutes):

- **☐ Total income received this week (gross before fees when possible)**
- **☐ Transfer your Tax % into the Tax Set-Aside bucket**
- **☐ Transfer your Profit/Reserve % into Profit/Reserve**
- **☐ Keep enough in Operating to cover upcoming bills**

- ☐ Move the planned amount into Owner Pay (even if small—consistency matters)
- ☐ Record everything in this tracker (income + expenses + notes)

Step 4 — The "Tax-Proof" Rule for Freelancers

Your tax bill is not a surprise. It's a bill you didn't fund.

The Tax Set-Aside Bucket is NOT for:

- new gear "because I needed it"
- groceries "because it was a slow month"
- a vacation "because I worked hard"

It's for taxes. Period.

Quarterly habit (recommended):

- Review your totals
- Estimate what you may owe
- Pay quarterly estimates if required
- Adjust your tax % if you are short or if income changed

Step 5 — Reality Check (Fees + Mixed Use)

Contractors get hit with two common money leaks:

1) Platform/processing fees

Track income as gross when possible, then track fees as an expense.
(If you only see net payouts, track what you can—just be consistent.)

2) Mixed personal/business spending

Phone, internet, vehicle, home office, equipment—many are mixed-use.
Track the expense and note the business purpose and the business-use portion.

Simple note examples:

- "Adobe – editing + client projects"

- **"Phone – business use portion"**
- **"Ring light – video production setup"**
- **"Mileage – client shoot travel"**

The Freelancer Money Map Worksheet (Print-Friendly)

A) Your Income Sources (check all that apply)

- **☐ Client work**
- **☐ Platform payouts**
- **☐ Sponsorships / brand deals**
- **☐ Affiliate income**
- **☐ Digital products / downloads**
- **☐ Tips / bonuses / royalties**
- **Other: ___________________**

B) Your 3–5 Buckets

Income Landing: _________________________
Tax Set-Aside: __________________________
Operating: _____________________________
Owner Pay: _____________________________
Profit/Reserve: _________________________

C) Your Starter Split Percentages

Tax Set-Aside:	**_____%**
Operating:	**_____%**
Owner Pay:	**_____%**
Profit/Reserve:	**_____%**
Total must equal	**100%.**

D) Your "Slow Month" Protection Plan

Minimum monthly operating bills:	**$________**
Minimum monthly personal needs (owner pay):	**$________**
Target buffer amount (1 month):	**$________**
Target buffer amount (2–3 months):	**$________**

E) Your Weekly Money Map Day

Day of week: _______________
Time: _____________________

Quick Example (How This Looks in Real Life)

If you receive $5,000 this month and your splits are:

- **30% Tax**
- **40% Operating**
- **10% Profit/Reserve**
- **20% Owner Pay**

Then:

- **Tax Set-Aside: $1,500**
- **Operating: $2,000**
- **Profit/Reserve: $500**
- **Owner Pay: $1,000**

Now you're not *hoping* you can pay taxes later—you have already funded them.

The Point of the Money Map

This isn't about being fancy. It's about being free.

When you consistently run this map, you get:

- **fewer tax surprises**
- **cleaner records**
- **smoother months**
- **less anxiety**
- **and a business that feels like a business—not a financial improv show**

FREELANCER AND INDEPENDENT CONTRACTOR SPECIFIC EXPENSE CATEGORIES CHEAT SHEET

Use this guide to categorize expenses fast, keep clean records, and make Schedule C prep easier.

This cheat sheet is designed for freelancers and independent contractors who file (or may need to file) Schedule C. The goal is simple: track expenses in a way that makes sense later—especially when you're handing totals to a tax pro or preparing your own return.

How to use this page:
When you log an expense in this book, choose the closest category below and write a short "business purpose" note when needed. That one note can be the difference between a clean deduction and an expense you can't defend.

Reminder: This tracker helps you stay organized. It does not replace professional tax advice. Tax rules vary by situation and can change.

The Categories (Freelancer / Independent Contractor Focus)

1) Advertising & Marketing

Expenses to find clients and keep your pipeline full.

- Business cards, flyers, brochures
- Website design costs (if paid as a service)
- Online ads (Google, Facebook, etc.)
- Networking event fees
- Portfolio printing or presentation materials
- Branding services (logo design, brand strategy)

Good note examples: "Google ad – lead generation," "Portfolio print – client meeting."

2) Office Supplies & Small Equipment

Consumable items and low-cost tools used in your work.

- Printer ink/paper

- Pens, folders, notebooks
- Small office tools and accessories
- Shipping supplies *only if used to deliver business materials/documents*
- Basic work-related supplies

Good note: "Printer ink – invoices and client packets."

3) Computer, Software & Subscriptions

Tools you pay for to do the work.

- Cloud storage (Dropbox, Google Drive upgrades)
- Microsoft 365 / Google Workspace
- Adobe, design tools, PDF tools
- Scheduling systems, project management tools
- Accounting/bookkeeping software
- Website hosting fees and domain renewals
- Business email service

Good note: "QuickBooks – bookkeeping," "Domain renewal – business website."

4) Contract Labor / Subcontractors

When you pay others to help you deliver services.

- Bookkeeper
- Virtual assistant
- Graphic designer
- Web developer
- Copywriter
- Specialist subcontractors (as part of client deliverables)

Compliance note (important): For U.S. contractors you pay, you typically want a W-9 on file before payment and accurate totals for possible 1099 reporting.

Good note: "VA support – scheduling & admin."

5) Professional Services

Experts you pay to keep your business compliant and operating well.

- Tax preparation fees
- Tax planning / consulting
- Legal consultations and document preparation
- Business formation filings (paid to a provider)
- Professional consulting tied to your existing business

Good note: "Tax planning session," "Contract review."

6) Business Insurance

Policies tied to operating the business.

- Professional liability / E&O insurance (if applicable)
- Business liability insurance
- Business property/equipment coverage (if separately billed)

7) Phone & Internet (Business Portion)

Often mixed-use. Track the business portion consistently.

- Cell phone plan (business use portion)
- Internet service (business use portion)
- Mobile hotspot (if used for work)

Best practice: Decide on a reasonable business-use percentage and stick with it (and note it once in your "how you track" section).

Good note: "Phone – 70% business use."

8) Travel, Mileage, Parking & Tolls (Business Only)

Transportation costs tied to work.

- Business mileage (client visits, work errands, business meetings)
- Parking fees while working
- Tolls
- Business-related rideshare/taxi
- Airfare/lodging when travel is primarily for business

Good note: "Mileage – client meeting," "Parking – onsite service call."

9) Meals (Use Carefully)

This category is frequently abused. You will learn to document it clearly.

- Meals that qualify under business rules (business purpose + who you met with)

Best note format: "Meal with [Name/Company] – discussed [business purpose]."

10) Rent, Coworking & Workspace Fees

If you pay for a workspace beyond your home.

- Coworking membership
- Office rent
- Meeting room rental
- Studio/office space fees (business use)

11) Education, Training & Professional Dues

Training that supports your current business (not a new career).

- Industry certifications related to current services
- Continuing education

- Professional memberships and dues
- Conferences or workshops tied to your work

Good note: "CE course – required for credential."

12) Banking & Processing Fees

Small fees that add up.

- Bank account fees
- Merchant account fees
- Credit card processing fees
- Wire/transfer fees
- Business credit card annual fee (if clearly business-related)

13) Licenses & Regulatory Fees

Fees required to legally operate.

- Business license fees
- Annual report filing fees
- Local permits required for your business

The "Don't Guess" List (Most Common Freelancer Problem Areas)

Mixed-use expenses

These often require business-use tracking and short notes:

- Phone
- Internet
- Vehicle
- Home office expenses
- Computer equipment used personally and professionally

Equipment vs supplies

If it's a bigger purchase that lasts (computer, printer, major equipment), track it clearly and flag it for your tax pro—handling may differ.

Meals

Meals can be deductible in limited situations. If you can't clearly explain who + business purpose, leave it out or ask your tax pro.

Business-Purpose Notes You Can Copy

- **"Client work"**
- **"Admin & operations"**
- **"Project delivery"**
- **"Client meeting"**
- **"Business development"**
- **"Business travel"**
- **"Required professional compliance"**

Bottom Line

If you do these three things consistently, you're ahead of most freelancers:

1. **Track income you receive**
2. **Track expenses by category**
3. **Add brief notes where needed**

SUBSCRIPTIONS & SOFTWARE TRACKER

(Part 1 — Why this matters)

If you're a freelancer, subscriptions are where your deductions quietly leak out of your life.

You sign up for:

- **an editing tool,**
- **a design tool,**
- **a scheduling tool,**
- **cloud storage,**
- **a website platform,**
- **an email service,**
- **a course platform,**
- **a link-in-bio tool...**

...and six months later you don't even remember what half of them are for.

This section fixes that.

Two goals

1. **Capture every recurring cost so you don't miss deductions.**
2. **Prevent "subscription creep" (you know—paying for five tools that do the same job).**

Quick rule for Freelancers

If a subscription supports your end product or enables delivery for services rendered, marketing, or business operations, it belongs here.

Common subscription (examples)

- **Editing: Adobe, Final Cut, CapCut Pro, Descript, Microsoft**
- **Design: Canva Pro, Adobe Express**
- **Scheduling: Later, Buffer, Metricool**
- **Stock assets: Shutterstock, Envato Elements, Creative Market**

- **Cloud storage: Dropbox, Google Drive, iCloud storage plans**
- **Website: domain + hosting, Squarespace, Wix, WordPress plugins**
- **Email: ConvertKit, Mailchimp**
- **Admin: bookkeeping tools, invoicing tools**

Quick monthly habit (30 seconds)

At the end of each month, scan your statements and add any new subscription here. If you don't, you'll "forget" them until tax time...which is not the moment you want surprises.

SUBSCRIPTIONS & SOFTWARE TRACKER

(Part 2 — Subscription sanity check)

This page is the difference between "organized" and "overpaying."

Freelancers often get stuck paying for tools they no longer use because:

- **the subscription renews automatically,**
- **the charge name is vague,**
- **the tool was for a one-time project,**
- **or you replaced it and forgot to cancel the old one.**

Quarterly clean-up checklist (use this 4 times a year)

☐ Do I still use this?
☐ Is there a cheaper plan that does what I need?
☐ Am I paying twice for the same function?
☐ Is this business-only or mixed-use?
☐ If mixed-use, what's my reasonable business percentage?

Mixed-use examples (be honest and consistent)

- **Cloud storage used for family + business**
- **Phone apps used for personal + business**
- **Streaming services used "sometimes for research"**
  If it's mixed, note your business percentage and keep that percentage consistent year to year unless something changes.

Profit increasing ideas:

Is an annual subscription less expensive than monthly for longer term tools?

Will paying for a lifetime subscription make more sense to build profitability?

Quick note

This isn't just tax planning. It's profit planning.
The easiest money you'll ever "earn" is canceling what you don't need.

Quick Rules (Freelancer-Specific)

- **If it's used for client work, operations, scheduling, invoicing, storage, communication, or professional compliance—track it here.**
- **If it's mixed-use (you use it personally too), note that and track the business-use percentage in the Notes column.**
- **If the subscription is annual, write the renewal month in big letters so you don't get surprised.**

"Find the Money Leaks" Mini Review (Monthly)

Once a month, take 3 minutes and answer:

- **Do I pay for two tools that do the same thing? ☐ Yes ☐ No**
- **Do I have anything I haven't used in 60 days? ☐ Yes ☐ No**
- **Do I have any annual renewals coming up that I should cancel now? ☐ Yes ☐ No**

Optional: Subscription Business-Use % Notes (If Needed)

Use this format when something is partly personal:

- **"Used ~70% for business / 30% personal"**
- **"Business only"**
- **"Personal only — remove from business totals"**

WORKSHEET: RECURRING SUBSCRIPTIONS LIST

(Track monthly and annual subscriptions in one place.)

Tax Year: _________ Business Name/Brand: ___________________________________

Subscription / Service	What it's for (Business Purpose)	Monthly or Annual	Amount	Renewal Date	Paid Through (card/PayPal /etc.)	Notes (Price Changes, Bundles, Cancellation)

WORKSHEET: SUBSCRIPTION REVIEW (QUARTERLY)

Quarter: ☐ Q1 ☐ Q2 ☐ Q3 ☐ Q4 Date Reviewed: ___________

Subscription	Keep / Cancel / Downgrade	Why Action Taken	Date Effective

BRAND DEALS & SPONSORSHIP JOB TRACKER

(Part 1 — Track each deal like a mini-client project)

Brand deals are where freelancers get into trouble—because it's not just "money."

It's often:

- **a contract,**
- **deliverables,**
- **deadlines,**
- **content usage rights,**
- **products shipped to you,**
- **reimbursable expenses,**
- **partial payments,**
- **performance bonuses,**
- **and late payouts.**

If you track brand deals like a real project, you protect yourself.

Why this belongs in an expense logbook

Because brand deals create:

- **income (cash)**
- **non-cash compensation (product)**
- **expenses (software, supplies, travel, shipping, software, subcontractors)**
- **timing issues (money earned vs money deposited)**

This tracker keeps it clean.

Freelancer Reality Checks

1) If it isn't written down, it's a misunderstanding.
Even a simple email confirmation of fee + deliverables beats "we discussed it on a call."

2) Don't confuse "exposure" with payment.
If you're paid, track it as income. If you're not paid, it isn't income—don't invent bookkeeping problems.

3) Deposits and milestone payments reduce late-pay risk.
If a client has a habit of paying slowly, structure payment terms accordingly next time.

4) Keep your paperwork.
Contracts, invoices, emails, and proof of delivery matter if there's ever a dispute—or if you're reconciling income at tax time.

WORKSHEET: SPONSORSHIP / BRAND DEAL TRACKER

(Use one worksheet per deal.)

Brand/Company: **Contact Name:**

Email/Phone: **Contract Signed Date:**

Campaign Name: **Platform(s):**

Deliverables (what you agreed to create)

☐ Instagram Post ☐ Reels ☐ Stories ☐ TikTok ☐ YouTube Short ☐ YouTube Video ☐ Live

☐ Blog ☐ UGC (not posted) ☐ Other: ____________________

Deliverable details (include dates):

____

____

Payment Details

Total fee: $____________ **Payment terms:** ☐ Upfront ☐ Net 15 ☐ Net 30 ☐ Other: __________

Payment method: ☐ ACH ☐ PayPal ☐ Check ☐ Other: ______________________________

Payment Schedule / Date Received:

- Date: ____________ Amount: $____________
- Date: ____________ Amount: $____________

Product Received (if any)

Product Received: ☐ Yes ☐ No

If yes, describe: ____

Estimated value (if known): $ ______________ Date Received: __________________

Reimbursable Expenses

Expenses you can bill back (if allowed):

____

Reimbursed? ☐ Yes ☐ No **Date Reimbursed:** ______________ **Amount: $** ____________

BRAND DEALS & SPONSORSHIP JOB TRACKER

(Part 2 — Usage rights, compliance, and proof)

Freelancers don't lose money only from "bad deals."

They lose money from unclear terms and missing proof.

This page helps you keep what matters in one place.

Usage rights (this is where people get burned)

Usage rights answer questions like:

- **Can the brand run your content as an ad?**
- **For how long?**
- **On what platforms?**
- **Can they edit it?**
- **Can they reuse it forever?**

If you don't track this, you can accidentally give away value.

Year-End Cleanup (Makes 1099 Season Easier)

At the end of the year, review this tracker and confirm:

- **Every job marked "Delivered" has a corresponding paid date**
- **Unpaid invoices are clearly flagged**
- **Your recorded income matches your deposits**
- **Client contact details are complete**

AFFILIATE & LINK REVENUE TRACKING

Quick Rules

1) Track what you *earned* and what you *received*

Affiliate programs often pay late, batch payments, or apply adjustments later. That's why "earned period" and "deposit date" both matter.

2) Don't ignore small deposits

Ten $17 deposits are still income—and they add up faster than you think.

3) Record adjustments honestly

Returns and chargebacks happen. Log them so your totals stay accurate.

4) Keep supporting records

At minimum, save:

- monthly program statements (PDFs or screenshots)
- payout confirmations
- bank deposit proof (if needed for reconciliation)

(Why your affiliate numbers never match your deposits)

Affiliate income is one of the messiest freelancer income streams because it's full of timing issues and adjustments.

You can do everything right and still see:

- payout delays (you "earned it" this month, it pays next month),
- returns and reversals (someone returns the item later),
- minimum payout thresholds (no payout until you hit $X),
- "pending" vs "approved" commissions,
- processors batching deposits together.

So don't try to force it into a perfect little box. Use a simple system that works.

The goal

Your goal is to be able to say, confidently:

"This is what I earned, these are the adjustments, and this is what I actually received."

That's it. That's clean.

What to save (quick habit)

☐ Screenshot/download monthly affiliate statement
☐ Save payout confirmation email (if you get one)
☐ Note any large reversals (so it doesn't look like "missing income" later)

If you use multiple affiliate platforms

That's normal. Just keep each program listed here and you'll be able to reconcile deposits without guessing.

WORKSHEET: AFFILIATE PAYOUT RECONCILIATION

(Use one per program, per month—OR one sheet per month with multiple programs.)

Month: ____________________

Affiliate Program	Period Covered	Gross Commissions	Adjustments (returns/reversals)	Net Approved	Payout Received	Deposit Date	Notes

Year-End Wrap-Up Checklist

Before tax filing:

- **☐ Confirm each affiliate program listed in the master list**
- **☐ Total net affiliate income for the year**
- **☐ Confirm deposits match your totals (or note timing differences)**
- **☐ Save year-end statements from each platform/program**

MARKETING & PROMOTION SPEND

Marketing spend is one of those categories that can either be your best investment or a slow leak you don't notice until you're wondering why the bank balance feels offended.

This section helps you track marketing and promotion costs in a way that answers three questions:

1. **What did I spend?**
2. **What was it for?**
3. **Did it bring in work—or just make me feel busy?**

You don't need a fancy system. You need a consistent one.

What Counts as Marketing & Promotion for Freelancers/Independent Contractors

Use this category for expenses intended to get clients, retain clients, or support client acquisition.

Common examples:

- **Website costs (design services, hosting, domain renewal)**
- **SEO tools/services, directory listings**
- **Online advertising (Google, social ads, local digital ads)**
- **Branding services (logo design, brand strategy)**
- **Business cards, brochures, printed materials**
- **Networking event fees, professional mixers (admission fees)**
- **Proposal tools, scheduling tools, CRM tools *if used primarily for lead generation/sales***
- **Email marketing platform fees (client outreach/newsletters)**
- **Referral thank-you gifts (reasonable + documented)**

Best practice: If you can't explain how it connects to getting/keeping clients, don't force it into "marketing."

What Usually Does *Not* Belong Here

(If you're unsure, track it anyway and flag it for your tax pro—but don't casually toss it into marketing.)

- **Personal clothing or "looking professional" purchases**
- **Personal grooming**
- **Entertainment that isn't clearly business-related**
- **Random "business inspiration" spending with no clear purpose**
- **Reality: "Spent $___ and learned what not to do." (Still useful.)**

WORKSHEET: PROMO SPEND + OUTCOME NOTES

(Simple tracking + light performance notes.)

Month/Period: ________________________

Date	Platform / Vendor	What you paid for	Amount	Business purpose	Outcome notes (optional)

Campaign Tracker

(Track the Stuff You Expect to Produce Results)
OPTIONAL ONLY IF APPLIES TO YOUR WORK

Use this when you spend money with a specific goal: more inquiries, more consultation calls, more signed contracts.

Campaign Name	Start Date	End Date	Channel (Ads / Email / Referral / Networking / Website)	Goal (Calls/Leads/Clients)	Budget	Actual Spend	Lead Generated	Clients Won	Notes (What worked / didn't)

Reality check: "Leads" are different from income generating "clients." Track both.

Monthly Marketing Budget vs. Actual (Keeps You Honest)

Month	Budgeted Marketing Spend	Actual Marketing Spend	Difference (- / +)	What You Spent It On (Short)	Was it Worth Repeating? (Y/ N)
Jan					
Feb					
Mar					
Apr					
May					
Jun					
Jul					
Aug					
Sep					
Oct					
Nov					
Dec					

LEAD SOURCE TRACKER

(Where Your Work Actually Comes From)

OPTIONAL ONLY IF APPLIES TO YOUR WORK

This is the page most freelancers wish they'd used sooner. over time, this shows you what to fund—and what to stop funding.

Date Inquiry Received	Lead Source (Referral/Website /Directory/Ad/Networking/Repeat Client)	Who Referred / Where Found You	Service Requested	Quote Sent? (Y/N)	Won the Client? (Y/N)	Notes

Simple ROI Check (No Math Degree Required)

At the end of each month or quarter, answer:

- **What did I spend on marketing? $________**
- **How many leads did I get? ________**
- **How many became paying clients? ________**
- **Total revenue from those clients (so far): $________**
- **Keep / Change / Stop: ________________________**

If you don't track this, marketing becomes a hobby. And hobbies are wonderful—just not deductible the way you want them to be.

One Rule That Saves Money

Don't keep paying for marketing you won't measure.
You don't need perfection. You need a basic "Did it work?" review.

PROJECT MATERIALS/CLIENT SUPPLIES / JOB INPUTS

(Part 1 — How to track without it looking like personal shopping)

This is one of the biggest danger zones for contractors —because the receipts often come from normal stores.

Target. Amazon. Walmart. Home Depot. Sephora. Best Buy.

The IRS doesn't care where you shop.

They care whether it was ordinary and necessary for your business and whether you can explain it.

The #1 rule: write the business purpose

Don't write "Amazon." Write what it actually was.

Examples:

- **"Printing supplies"**
- **"Prop items for product demo video"**
- **"Backdrop and set pieces for filming area"**
- **"Wardrobe for paid brand shoot (business use)"**
- **"Packaging supplies for merch shipments"**
- **"Makeup/hair for on-camera paid campaign (if genuinely business-related)"**

Mixed-use is real

Some things are clearly business. Some are clearly personal. Some are mixed.

If something is mixed-use:

- **track it,**
- **document your business purpose,**
- **and be reasonable about the portion you claim.**

You don't need to be perfect. You need to be consistent and defensible.

WORKSHEET: PROPS / SAMPLES / WARDROBE / SET PURCHASE

(Use this when a purchase could look personal unless explained.)

Tax Year: ____________________ **Freelancer Brand:** ______________________________

Date	Store / Vendor	Item Purchased	Amount	Category (prop/wardrobe/set /etc.)	Business Purpose (write it plainly)	% Business Use	Notes

PROPS, SAMPLES, WARDROBE, SET DESIGN & "CONTENT PURCHASES"- OPTIONAL ONLY IF APPLIES TO YOUR WORK

(Part 2 — Samples, product received, and returns)

Freelancers may receive products in three different ways:

1. **You bought it (normal expense)**
2. **You were sent it (non-cash compensation or PR)**
3. **You were reimbursed (expense + reimbursement trail)**

These aren't the same thing. Track them cleanly so you're not guessing later.

Product sent to you (PR or brand deal)

If a company sends you product, track:

- **what it was,**
- **when you received it,**
- **and what you delivered (if anything).**

It might be taxable, or it might not—depending on the facts. Your job is to keep a clean record so your tax pro can classify it correctly.

If you traded services (barter) or received a non-cash benefit, track it here the same way—what you received, when, and what you delivered.

Your tax pro will decide. Your job is to keep a clean record.
Returns and exchanges

If you return something you logged as an expense:

- **note it,**
- **and keep proof of refund or store credit.**

Refunds and chargebacks are not always normal in a freelancer business. What matters is that your records reflect your business operations reality.

WORKSHEET: PRODUCT RECEIVED / PR / SAMPLES LOG

(Use this for non-cash products and PR packages.)

Date Received	Brand/Company	Item(s) Received	Estimated Value (if known)	Was content required? (Y/N)	Deliverables / Notes

CLIENT PROJECT COSTS & REIMBURSABLE TRACKER

Use this tracker when expenses are tied to a specific client job. This is the easiest way to:

- **keep project costs from getting lost in your general expense log**
- **track reimbursables (so you don't "forget to bill yourself back")**
- **see what each job truly cost you to deliver**

Tip: If a cost is tied to a job, log it here and (if you want clean totals later) in your main expense log as well. If you hate double-entry, log it here only—just be consistent.

Project Overview (Fill Once Per Job)

- **Client / Company: ________________________**
- **Project / Job Name: ______________________**
- **Contract Date: __________ Start Date: __________ Due Date: __________**
- **Fee Agreed (Labor): $__________**
- **Reimbursables Allowed? ☐ Yes ☐ No**
- **If Yes: Cap / Limits: ____**
- **Payment Terms: ☐ Upfront ☐ Net 15 ☐ Net 30 ☐ Milestones ☐ Other: _______**

Job Cost + Reimbursables Log

Quick Job Profit Snapshot (Optional but powerful)

Date	Expense / Cost Item	Vendor / Payee	Type (Direct / Reimbursable / Subcontractor)	Amount	Bill to Client? (Y/N)	Billed Date	Invoice #	Reimbursed / Paid Date	Notes (business purpose / what it was for)

- **Fee Agreed (Labor): $________**
- **Total Job Costs (from log): $________**
- **Estimated Net Before Taxes: $________**

(This is not a tax calculation. It's a reality check.)

RETAINERS & DEPOSITS TRACKER (Cash-Basis Clarity)

(Use this when money arrives before the work is fully delivered.)

Date Received	Client / Company	Amount Received	Type: Retainer / Deposit / Advance Payment / Other	Refundable? Yes / No / Partial (Notes)	Purpose / What it covers (one line)	Applied to Invoice # / Date(s) (when you apply it)	Remaining Unapplied Balance	Notes

"Keep retainers/deposits tied to the invoice(s) they were applied to—this prevents double-counting income or 'missing' payments."

INVOICE AND PAYMENT TRACKER

Freelancers don't "get paid." They get paid when they track and follow up. This page keeps your invoices, due dates, and collections in one place.

Invoice & Collections Log

Clients / Company	Project / Job	Invoice #	Amount Invoiced	Terms (Net 15 / 30/ etc.)	Due Date	Paid Date	Amount Received	Method (ACH / Check / etc.)	Balance Due	Follow-Up Dates / Notes

Follow-up note examples:

- **"Sent reminder email 2/5"**
- **"Client requested revised invoice 3/10"**
- **"Partial payment received"**

ACCOUNTS RECEIVABLE + INVOICE AGING SNAPSHOT

(Use weekly—this is your "collections dashboard.")

Invoice #	Client / Company	Amount	Due Date	Paid Date (blank if unpaid)	Status						Follow-up Date	Notes	Aging (Past Due)			
					Sent	Due	Over due	Partial	Paid	Write off			0-30	31-60	61-90	90+

"If it's overdue, schedule the follow-up date. Freelancers don't get paid by hoping."

Mixed-Use Expense Percent Tracker

Some expenses are partly business and partly personal. This page helps you track the business-use percentage you're using and apply it consistently.

Use this for common mixed-use items like phone, internet, vehicle, home office costs, and equipment used for both personal and business.

Mixed-Use Percent Log

Mixed-Use Item	Service / Asset	Business-Use %	How You Determined It (simple explanation)	Start Date	Review Date	Notes
Phone	__________	___%	______________________	___	____	____________
Internet	__________	___%	______________________	___	____	____________
Vehicle	__________	___%	______________________	___	____	____________
Home Office	__________	___%	______________________	___	____	____________
Equipment	__________	___%	______________________	___	____	____________

Reality rule: If you can't explain it in one sentence, it's too fuzzy. Tighten the method.

FEES, PROCESSING FEES, CHARGEBACKS & "WHY MY DEPOSITS DON'T MATCH"

...t card payments or get paid through a payment processor, your ...n won't match your invoices. That's normal. It's also the fastest way ... of income (and deductions) if you don't track it on purpose.

The Most Common Reasons Deposits Don't Match

- Processing fees withheld (Stripe/PayPal/Square/etc.)
- Invoice software fees or "instant payout" fees
- Partial payments (deposit now, balance later)
- Client refunds (full or partial)
- Chargebacks/disputes and chargeback fees
- Timing differences (payment received Friday, deposited Monday)
- Bundled deposits (multiple invoices paid, one combined deposit)
- Withheld reserves (processor holds funds temporarily for risk/review)

Your job is to track:

1. what the client paid (gross)
2. what you actually received (net)
3. what happened to the difference (fees/refunds/chargebacks)

A) Payment Processor Monthly Summary (Fast Reconciliation)

Use one line per processor per month.

B) Deposit Match-Up Log (When One Deposit Covers Multiple Invoices)

Use this when deposits are bundled, split, or confusing.

WORKSHEET: MONTHLY DEPOSIT RECONCILIATION

(Use one per month OR one per platform—whatever keeps you consistent.)

Month: ________________ Tax Year: __________

Platform / Processor	Gross Sales / Earnings	Platform / Processing Fees	Refunds	Chargebacks	Other Adjustments	Net Deposited	Deposit Date(s)	Notes

Explanation examples:

- **"Two invoices bundled into one deposit"**
- **"Instant payout fee deducted"**
- **"Refund issued same week"**
- **"Chargeback fee withheld"**

Chargeback & Dispute Tracker (Because It's Not Just the Lost Payment)

Chargebacks can cost you the payment plus a fee. Track them cleanly.

Date Opened	Client / Customer	Invoice #	Amount Disputed	Reason (as stated)	Response Due Date	Outcome (Won / Lost)	Amount Recovered	Fees Charged	Notes

Quick "Deposit Doesn't Match" Checklist

When you see a mismatch, run this checklist before you waste an hour:

- **☐ Was there a processing fee?**
- **☐ Was it a partial payment?**
- **☐ Was it multiple invoices bundled?**
- **☐ Was there a refund or adjustment?**
- **☐ Did the processor delay/hold a portion?**
- **☐ Did you pay for "instant payout"?**
- **☐ Did the client pay on one date but it deposited later?**

Where These Numbers Go in Your Book

- Fees → track as an expense (Processing/Banking Fees or similar)
- Chargeback fees → track as an expense
- Refunds → track as a reduction tied to the original income (note it clearly)
- Gross income → belongs in your income tracking

TRAVEL: WHAT WORKS, WHAT DOESN'T, AND HOW TO LOG IT

Travel deductions aren't hard because the math is hard. They're hard because the IRS cares about purpose, documentation, and whether the trip was truly business.

This section gives you practical guardrails so you can track travel confidently—without getting "creative" in ways that come back to bite you.

Rule #1: If you can't explain the business purpose in one sentence, don't deduct it.

1) Two Types of Travel You'll Track

A) Local business travel (usually mileage + parking/tolls)

Driving from your home office/business base to:

- a client meeting
- a job site
- a coworking space/meeting room rented for business
- business errands that are ordinary and necessary

B) Travel "away from home" (overnight or long enough to need rest)

Trips where you're away from your tax home long enough that you reasonably need sleep/rest.
These require a clear business purpose and clean documentation.

2) What Works: Three Realistic Examples

Example 1 — Onsite client project (Works)

You travel to another city for two days to deliver contracted services (training, installation, consulting, project execution).

Why it works: The trip's primary purpose is business, tied to a paying client engagement, and you can document the schedule and deliverables.

Example 2 — Conference/required training tied to your current work (Works)

You attend a professional conference or continuing education directly related to your existing services (not a "someday I might do this" topic).

Why it works: The training supports your current business, and you can show registration, agenda, and proof of attendance.

Example 3 — Planned business development trip with documented meetings (Works)

You travel to meet two prospective clients and one referral partner, with pre-scheduled meetings and notes afterward.
Why it works: There's a clear plan, documented meetings, and a business objective—not vague "networking."

3) What Doesn't Work: Three Common Mistakes

Example 1 — "I answered emails while on vacation" (Doesn't work)

You take a personal trip and do a little work from the hotel.
Why it doesn't work: Answering emails doesn't convert a personal trip into a business trip.

Example 2 — "Networking" with no specifics (Doesn't work)

You travel "to network" but don't have meetings scheduled, no agenda, no client targets, no outcomes—just spending.
Why it doesn't work: Vague purpose + no documentation = weak deduction.

Example 3 — One business errand inside a mostly personal trip (Doesn't work)

You visit family for a week and stop by one potential client for 30 minutes.
Why it doesn't work: A small business activity doesn't transform an otherwise personal trip into deductible travel.

Reality check: If business is an afterthought, the deduction is shaky.

4) The One-Sentence Business Purpose Test

Write a sentence that would make sense to a third party six months later.

Good:

- "Traveled to Miami to deliver onsite consulting for Client X and complete project milestones."
- "Attended [Conference Name] for CE directly related to my bookkeeping practice."
- "Met with two prospective clients regarding contract work; meetings scheduled in advance."

Bad:

- "Business trip / networking."
- "Went to explore opportunities."
- "Worked while I was there."

5) How to Log It (Simple Templates)

A) Local Travel Log (Mileage + Parking/Tolls)

Date	Destination	Business Purpose (1 sentence)	Miles	Parking/Tolls	Notes

B) Overnight Travel Log (Trip Summary)

Destination: ____________________
Dates: ________ to __________

Primary business purpose (one sentence):

____

Business activities (what you did):

- ____
- ____
- ____

Who you met with (if applicable):

____

Expenses tracked (keep receipts):
☐ Transportation ☐ Lodging ☐ Parking/Tolls ☐ Other:

____

Notes (timing, schedule, anything that explains the trip):

____

____

6) Mixed Business + Personal Trips (Handle Carefully)

If a trip has both business and personal time, the safest approach is:

- **clearly separate business days and personal days**
- **document business meetings/activities**
- **track expenses that clearly match the business purpose**
- **avoid "blending" and hoping it works out later**

Bottom Line

Freelancers and independent contractors can absolutely have valid travel deductions—when the trip has a clear business purpose and your log supports the story.

MULTI-STATE WORK/TRAVEL/TRAVEL TRACKER

(lightweight recordkeeping)

Create this topic/page. This fits perfectly in the Travel section because it's specifically about "I forgot I worked in ___." Your Travel section already exists with daytrip and overnight logs.

State	Dates Worked	Traveled		Client / Company	City (Optional)	Type of work (onsite / remote / event / temp gig)	Notes (what you were doing, quick context)
		From	To				

"This is a memory tool, so you don't forget where you worked or traveled for jobs."

Mileage Log Book Referral (Optional)

Vehicle mileage must be tracked separately.

Any mileage log used should meet IRS recordkeeping requirements.

Please refer to your dedicated Mileage Log Book for all mileage-related deductions.

Deluxe version Mileage Log Book Titles on Amazon for consideration with IRS compliance helps with separate sections for business, medical, charitable and volunteer mileage included authored by A. Herrick:

Basic version Mileage Log Book Titles on Amazon with only business mileage logs included authored by A. Herrick:

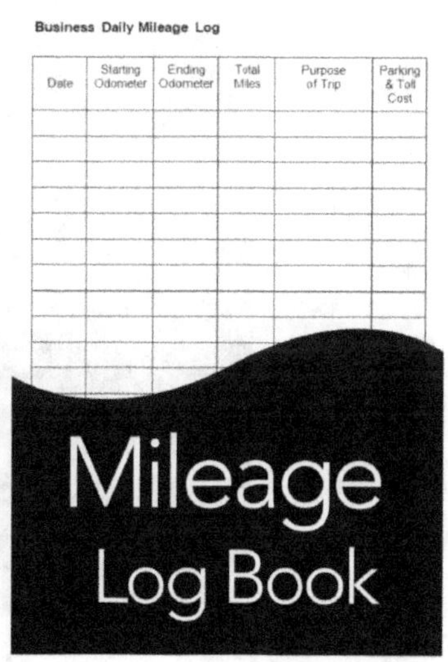

Schedule C Companion Reference (Optional)

For readers who want a clearer understanding of how Schedule C deductions work and what expense categories may apply to their business, you may find it helpful to reference *Self-Employed Taxes: Unleashing Schedule C Deductions.*

This companion book focuses on explaining the Schedule C form itself and how common deductions are treated under current tax law, while this record book is designed specifically for organizing and documenting your expenses. Used together, they can support better understanding and cleaner records.

IRS Category Definitions

Advertising: Costs for promoting your business such as flyers, business cards, and online ads.

Commissions and Fees: Payments made to non-employees for services provided.

Insurance: Business insurance premiums (excluding health).

Legal and Professional Services: Attorney fees, accounting fees, and consultant costs.

Office Expenses: Office supplies, postage, and small equipment under IRS thresholds.

Repairs and Maintenance: Upkeep of business property and equipment.

Supplies: Materials used in your business that are not included in inventory.

Taxes and Licenses: Business-related state, federal, and local taxes; permits and licenses.

Travel: Business travel expenses excluding meals.

Meals: Meals with clients or business-related meals (subject to IRS limits).

Utilities: Business portion of electricity, water, telecommunications, etc.

ANNUAL INSURANCE + LICENSE RENEWALS LOG

(simple yearly page)

	Coverage / License / Membership	Provider / Issuer	Policy or License # (optional)	Renewal Date	Amount Paid	Paid Date	Business Purpose (one line)	Notes (coverage limits, login info location, etc.)
General Liability								
E&O / Professional Liability								
Cyber coverage (if applicable)								
Bonding (if applicable)								
Local business license / permits								
Professional membership(s)								
Continuing education / required renewals								

MIXED-USE EXPENSES

Mixed-use expenses are the ones that are partly business and partly personal.

They're extremely common for freelancers and independent contractors—and they're also where people either (1) miss legitimate deductions or (2) claim things too aggressively and can't support them later.

This guide helps you track mixed-use expenses in a way that's reasonable, consistent, and defensible.

The goal: Use a method you can explain in plain English and apply the same way all year.

1) The Mixed-Use Rule (Simple Version)

If an expense has both business and personal use, you generally track only the business portion.

That means you need two things:

1. **a business-use percentage (or another clear method), and**
2. **a short explanation of how you arrived at it.**

If you can't explain it, it's too fuzzy.

2) The "Would I Buy This Without the Business?" Test

Ask yourself one honest question:

Would I still buy this if I didn't have the business?

- **If no, it's likely business-related (still document it).**
- **If yes, it's likely personal or mixed-use. Track only the business portion.**

This one question prevents most bad decisions.

3) The 5 Big Mixed-Use Categories for Freelancers/ICs

A) Phone (Cell Plan + Device)

Common business use: client calls, scheduling, email, navigation to meetings, business apps.
How to track: choose a reasonable business-use percentage and stick to it.

Good methods:

- **"I use this phone primarily for business during the work week—estimated 70% business."**
- **"I have a separate business line/app number—estimated 80% business."**

Document once: write your chosen percentage and method in your tracker, then apply it consistently.

B) Internet

Common business use: client communications, file uploads, invoicing, video calls, online research.
How to track: a percentage based on household use.

Reasonable method examples:

- **"Home internet supports business use weekdays; estimated 60% business."**
- **"Only two adults use internet; business is primary daytime use; estimated 50% business."**

C) Vehicle (Mileage / Auto Costs)

For most freelancers and independent contractors, mileage tracking is the cleanest method.

Business miles include:

- **driving to client sites/meetings**
- **driving to a coworking space for business**
- **business errands (bank, post office, supplies, shipping business documents)**

Business miles do NOT include:

- **commuting to a regular W-2 job**
- **personal errands**

- "I was thinking about business while driving"

What makes vehicle deductions defensible:
A mileage log with date, destination, purpose, and miles.

D) Home Office (if you qualify)

A home office can be a legitimate deduction, but the rules are specific. Two important principles:

1. The space generally needs to be used regularly and exclusively for business.
2. Track the costs cleanly and let your tax pro determine the method.

What you should track in this book:

- the dedicated work area (square footage or description)
- business-use percentage method (if applicable)
- related expenses you pay (rent, utilities, etc.—tracked consistently)

Avoid: trying to "force" a home office deduction if your workspace is truly shared personal space.

E) Equipment Used for Both Business and Personal

Examples: laptop, printer, tablet, phone, monitor.

Best practice:

- If it's truly mixed-use, choose a reasonable business-use percentage and document it.
- If it's primarily for business, say so and keep the explanation simple.

Good note examples:

- "Laptop used for business 80%—client work, invoicing, project delivery."
- "Printer used mainly for business documents—estimated 70% business."

4) The Consistency Rule (This Matters More Than People Think)

The IRS doesn't require you to be psychic. But they do expect you to be consistent.

Pick a method you can justify, then apply it:

- **all year**
- **across similar expenses**
- **with notes that match reality**

If your percentage changes dramatically, document why (new client load, new household use, changed work schedule, etc.).

5) Mixed-Use Expense Tracking Template (Copy This Into Your Book)

Use this format in your tracker pages:

Expense: ______________________

Business-use %: _____%

Method (one sentence): ____

When reviewed: _________ **(monthly/quarterly/yearly)**

This keeps your documentation clean and repeatable.

6) Quick "Usually Risky" List (Don't Get Cute)

These are common trouble areas for freelancers/ICs:

- **personal clothing labeled as "work clothes"**
- **meals without a clear business purpose and who/what/why**
- **travel where business is vague or minimal**
- **personal grooming framed as business**
- **"I need it to look professional" purchases without a real business tie**

If it's hard to explain without sounding defensive, it's probably not worth claiming.

7) Quick "Usually Legit" List (When Documented)

- **business portion of phone and internet**

- **mileage to client meetings and job sites**
- **software used to deliver services**
- **equipment used primarily for business**
- **home office *when it truly qualifies***

Bottom Line

Mixed-use deductions aren't about squeezing every possible dollar out of your life. They're about capturing the legitimate business portion of shared costs—with a method you can explain and defend.

CHART OF ACCOUNTS CHEAT SHEET

"What I bought" → "Where it goes" → "What to call it"

Use this page when you're not sure where an expense belongs. Pick the closest match, be consistent, and add a one-line note when needed.

What I bought / paid for	Where it goes (Category)	What to call it (Simple description)
Website hosting	Software & Subscriptions	"Website hosting"
Domain renewal	Software & Subscriptions	"Domain renewal"
Business email service	Software & Subscriptions	"Business email"
Cloud storage (Dropbox/Drive upgrade)	Software & Subscriptions	"Cloud storage"
Scheduling tool	Software & Subscriptions	"Scheduling software"
Invoice/payment platform fee	Banking/Processing Fees	"Processing fees"
Credit card processing fees	Banking/Processing Fees	"Card processing fees"
Bank service charge	Banking/Processing Fees	"Bank fees"
New laptop or computer	Equipment	"Computer equipment"
Printer/scanner	Equipment	"Office equipment"
Printer ink/paper	Office Supplies	"Office supplies"
Pens/notebooks/folders	Office Supplies	"Office supplies"
Client proposal printing	Project Costs (Job-related)	"Client deliverables printing"
Postage/courier for client documents	Project Costs (Job-related)	"Client document delivery"
Paid stock photo/font/license for a client project	Project Costs (Job-related)	"Project materials license"

What I bought / paid for	Where it goes (Category)	What to call it (Simple description)
Paid contractor to help on a client job	Project Costs (Subcontractor)	"Subcontractor – project support"
Bookkeeper	Professional Services	"Bookkeeping services"
Tax preparation	Professional Services	"Tax prep"
Legal consult/contract review	Professional Services	"Legal services"
Business insurance premium	Insurance	"Business insurance"
Coworking day pass	Rent/Workspace	"Coworking fee"
Office rent	Rent/Workspace	"Office rent"
Business cards	Advertising/Marketing	"Business cards"
Online ads	Advertising/Marketing	"Advertising"
Networking event admission	Advertising/Marketing	"Networking event fee"
Mileage to a client meeting	Travel/Mileage	"Business mileage"
Parking for a client visit	Travel/Mileage	"Parking"
Tolls while traveling for business	Travel/Mileage	"Tolls"
Cell phone plan (business portion)	Mixed-Use (Phone/Internet)	"Phone – business portion"
Home internet (business portion)	Mixed-Use (Phone/Internet)	"Internet – business portion"
Business meal with a client/prospect	Meals (Document carefully)	"Business meal – client meeting"
Course/conference for current services	Education/Training	"Professional training"
Professional dues	Education/Training	"Professional dues"

What I bought / paid for	Where it goes (Category)	What to call it (Simple description)
Business license/annual filing	Licenses/Fees	"Business license"

Two rules that keep this clean

1. Job-specific costs go to "Project Costs" (especially reimbursables and subcontractor help).
2. Fees that reduce deposits belong in "Banking/Processing Fees," so your income doesn't look "wrong."

WORKSHEET: "WHAT WAS THIS?" RECEIPT NOTES

(Use this for vague receipts like

Date	Vendor	Amount	What it was (plain English)	Category Label	Business pupose note

Sample Completed Entry

Date	1/13	1/19	1/10	1/15	1/15	1/15	1/19	
Vendor or Payee	Johnsons	Wallmart	AI Expo	AA	Marriott	RS DOL	Ofcmax	
Description	Laptop Repair	Office Supplies	Booth	June Air	June Hotel	License	Supplies	Page Total
Advertising			1500					$ 1,500.00
Commissions & Fees								
Employee Benefit Programs								
Insurance -Other								
Business Interest								
Legal & Professional Services								
Office Expenses		157.18					25.17	$ 182.35
Pension & Profit Sharing								
Rent or Lease								
Repairs & Maintenance	87.14							$ 87.14
Supplies								
Taxes & Licenses						250		$ 250.00
Travel				987.24	671.5			$ 1,658.74
Meals								
Business Utilities Only								
Miscellaneous								

Note #1:Home Office, Contractor payments, Depreciated Items and Self-Employed Health Insurance are summarized on dedicated pages a separate section of this book.

Note #2: Track your business miles and vehicle expenses in a separate mileage log to ensure accurate reporting and to determine the best deduction method for your situation.

Note #3: Cost of Goods is in another dedicated section of the book.

Note #4: I suggest you use a payroll program if you have employees that will require issuing a W2 for wages to ensure accurate reporting.

Date								
Vendor or Payee								
Description								Page Total
Advertising								
Commissions & Fees								
Employee Benefit Programs								
Insurance -Other								
Business Interest								
Legal & Professional Services								
Office Expenses								
Pension & Profit Sharing								
Rent or Lease								
Repairs & Maintenance								
Supplies								
Taxes & Licenses								
Travel								
Meals								
Business Utilities Only								
Miscellaneous								

Note #1:Home Office, Contractor payments, Depreciated Items and Self-Employed Health Insurance are summarized on dedicated pages a separate section of this book.

Note #2: Track your business miles and vehicle expenses in a separate mileage log to ensure accurate reporting and to determine the best deduction method for your situation.

Note #3: Cost of Goods is in another dedicated section of the book.

Note #4: I suggest you use a payroll program if you have employees that will require issuing a W2 for wages to ensure accurate reporting.

Date								
Vendor or Payee								
Description								Page Total
Advertising								
Commissions & Fees								
Employee Benefit Programs								
Insurance -Other								
Business Interest								
Legal & Professional Services								
Office Expenses								
Pension & Profit Sharing								
Rent or Lease								
Repairs & Maintenance								
Supplies								
Taxes & Licenses								
Travel								
Meals								
Business Utilities Only								
Miscellaneous								

Note #1:Home Office, Contractor payments, Depreciated Items and Self-Employed Health Insurance are summarized on dedicated pages a separate section of this book.

Note #2: Track your business miles and vehicle expenses in a separate mileage log to ensure accurate reporting and to determine the best deduction method for your situation.

Note #3: Cost of Goods is in another dedicated section of the book.

Note #4: I suggest you use a payroll program if you have employees that will require issuing a W2 for wages to ensure accurate reporting.

Date								
Vendor or Payee								
Description								Page Total
Advertising								
Commissions & Fees								
Employee Benefit Programs								
Insurance -Other								
Business Interest								
Legal & Professional Services								
Office Expenses								
Pension & Profit Sharing								
Rent or Lease								
Repairs & Maintenance								
Supplies								
Taxes & Licenses								
Travel								
Meals								
Business Utilities Only								
Miscellaneous								

Note #1:Home Office, Contractor payments, Depreciated Items and Self-Employed Health Insurance are summarized on dedicated pages a separate section of this book.

Note #2: Track your business miles and vehicle expenses in a separate mileage log to ensure accurate reporting and to determine the best deduction method for your situation.

Note #3: Cost of Goods is in another dedicated section of the book.

Note #4: I suggest you use a payroll program if you have employees that will require issuing a W2 for wages to ensure accurate reporting.

Date								
Vendor or Payee								
Description								Page Total
Advertising								
Commissions & Fees								
Employee Benefit Programs								
Insurance -Other								
Business Interest								
Legal & Professional Services								
Office Expenses								
Pension & Profit Sharing								
Rent or Lease								
Repairs & Maintenance								
Supplies								
Taxes & Licenses								
Travel								
Meals								
Business Utilities Only								
Miscellaneous								

Note #1:Home Office, Contractor payments, Depreciated Items and Self-Employed Health Insurance are summarized on dedicated pages a separate section of this book.

Note #2: Track your business miles and vehicle expenses in a separate mileage log to ensure accurate reporting and to determine the best deduction method for your situation.

Note #3: Cost of Goods is in another dedicated section of the book.

Note #4: I suggest you use a payroll program if you have employees that will require issuing a W2 for wages to ensure accurate reporting.

Date								
Vendor or Payee								
Description								Page Total
Advertising								
Commissions & Fees								
Employee Benefit Programs								
Insurance -Other								
Business Interest								
Legal & Professional Services								
Office Expenses								
Pension & Profit Sharing								
Rent or Lease								
Repairs & Maintenance								
Supplies								
Taxes & Licenses								
Travel								
Meals								
Business Utilities Only								
Miscellaneous								

Note #1:Home Office, Contractor payments, Depreciated Items and Self-Employed Health Insurance are summarized on dedicated pages a separate section of this book.

Note #2: Track your business miles and vehicle expenses in a separate mileage log to ensure accurate reporting and to determine the best deduction method for your situation.

Note #3: Cost of Goods is in another dedicated section of the book.

Note #4: I suggest you use a payroll program if you have employees that will require issuing a W2 for wages to ensure accurate reporting.

Date								
Vendor or Payee								
Description								Page Total
Advertising								
Commissions & Fees								
Employee Benefit Programs								
Insurance -Other								
Business Interest								
Legal & Professional Services								
Office Expenses								
Pension & Profit Sharing								
Rent or Lease								
Repairs & Maintenance								
Supplies								
Taxes & Licenses								
Travel								
Meals								
Business Utilities Only								
Miscellaneous								

Note #1:Home Office, Contractor payments, Depreciated Items and Self-Employed Health Insurance are summarized on dedicated pages a separate section of this book.

Note #2: Track your business miles and vehicle expenses in a separate mileage log to ensure accurate reporting and to determine the best deduction method for your situation.

Note #3: Cost of Goods is in another dedicated section of the book.

Note #4: I suggest you use a payroll program if you have employees that will require issuing a W2 for wages to ensure accurate reporting.

Date								
Vendor or Payee								
Description								Page Total
Advertising								
Commissions & Fees								
Employee Benefit Programs								
Insurance -Other								
Business Interest								
Legal & Professional Services								
Office Expenses								
Pension & Profit Sharing								
Rent or Lease								
Repairs & Maintenance								
Supplies								
Taxes & Licenses								
Travel								
Meals								
Business Utilities Only								
Miscellaneous								

Note #1:Home Office, Contractor payments, Depreciated Items and Self-Employed Health Insurance are summarized on dedicated pages a separate section of this book.

Note #2: Track your business miles and vehicle expenses in a separate mileage log to ensure accurate reporting and to determine the best deduction method for your situation.

Note #3: Cost of Goods is in another dedicated section of the book.

Note #4: I suggest you use a payroll program if you have employees that will require issuing a W2 for wages to ensure accurate reporting.

Date								
Vendor or Payee								
Description								Page Total
Advertising								
Commissions & Fees								
Employee Benefit Programs								
Insurance -Other								
Business Interest								
Legal & Professional Services								
Office Expenses								
Pension & Profit Sharing								
Rent or Lease								
Repairs & Maintenance								
Supplies								
Taxes & Licenses								
Travel								
Meals								
Business Utilities Only								
Miscellaneous								

Note #1:Home Office, Contractor payments, Depreciated Items and Self-Employed Health Insurance are summarized on dedicated pages a separate section of this book.

Note #2: Track your business miles and vehicle expenses in a separate mileage log to ensure accurate reporting and to determine the best deduction method for your situation.

Note #3: Cost of Goods is in another dedicated section of the book.

Note #4: I suggest you use a payroll program if you have employees that will require issuing a W2 for wages to ensure accurate reporting.

Date								
Vendor or Payee								
Description								Page Total
Advertising								
Commissions & Fees								
Employee Benefit Programs								
Insurance -Other								
Business Interest								
Legal & Professional Services								
Office Expenses								
Pension & Profit Sharing								
Rent or Lease								
Repairs & Maintenance								
Supplies								
Taxes & Licenses								
Travel								
Meals								
Business Utilities Only								
Miscellaneous								

Note #1:Home Office, Contractor payments, Depreciated Items and Self-Employed Health Insurance are summarized on dedicated pages a separate section of this book.

Note #2: Track your business miles and vehicle expenses in a separate mileage log to ensure accurate reporting and to determine the best deduction method for your situation.

Note #3: Cost of Goods is in another dedicated section of the book.

Note #4: I suggest you use a payroll program if you have employees that will require issuing a W2 for wages to ensure accurate reporting.

Date								
Vendor or Payee								
Description								Page Total
Advertising								
Commissions & Fees								
Employee Benefit Programs								
Insurance -Other								
Business Interest								
Legal & Professional Services								
Office Expenses								
Pension & Profit Sharing								
Rent or Lease								
Repairs & Maintenance								
Supplies								
Taxes & Licenses								
Travel								
Meals								
Business Utilities Only								
Miscellaneous								

Note #1:Home Office, Contractor payments, Depreciated Items and Self-Employed Health Insurance are summarized on dedicated pages a separate section of this book.

Note #2: Track your business miles and vehicle expenses in a separate mileage log to ensure accurate reporting and to determine the best deduction method for your situation.

Note #3: Cost of Goods is in another dedicated section of the book.

Note #4: I suggest you use a payroll program if you have employees that will require issuing a W2 for wages to ensure accurate reporting.

Date								
Vendor or Payee								
Description								Page Total
Advertising								
Commissions & Fees								
Employee Benefit Programs								
Insurance -Other								
Business Interest								
Legal & Professional Services								
Office Expenses								
Pension & Profit Sharing								
Rent or Lease								
Repairs & Maintenance								
Supplies								
Taxes & Licenses								
Travel								
Meals								
Business Utilities Only								
Miscellaneous								

Note #1:Home Office, Contractor payments, Depreciated Items and Self-Employed Health Insurance are summarized on dedicated pages a separate section of this book.

Note #2: Track your business miles and vehicle expenses in a separate mileage log to ensure accurate reporting and to determine the best deduction method for your situation.

Note #3: Cost of Goods is in another dedicated section of the book.

Note #4: I suggest you use a payroll program if you have employees that will require issuing a W2 for wages to ensure accurate reporting.

Date								
Vendor or Payee								
Description								Page Total
Advertising								
Commissions & Fees								
Employee Benefit Programs								
Insurance -Other								
Business Interest								
Legal & Professional Services								
Office Expenses								
Pension & Profit Sharing								
Rent or Lease								
Repairs & Maintenance								
Supplies								
Taxes & Licenses								
Travel								
Meals								
Business Utilities Only								
Miscellaneous								

Note #1:Home Office, Contractor payments, Depreciated Items and Self-Employed Health Insurance are summarized on dedicated pages a separate section of this book.

Note #2: Track your business miles and vehicle expenses in a separate mileage log to ensure accurate reporting and to determine the best deduction method for your situation.

Note #3: Cost of Goods is in another dedicated section of the book.

Note #4: I suggest you use a payroll program if you have employees that will require issuing a W2 for wages to ensure accurate reporting.

Date								
Vendor or Payee								
Description								Page Total
Advertising								
Commissions & Fees								
Employee Benefit Programs								
Insurance -Other								
Business Interest								
Legal & Professional Services								
Office Expenses								
Pension & Profit Sharing								
Rent or Lease								
Repairs & Maintenance								
Supplies								
Taxes & Licenses								
Travel								
Meals								
Business Utilities Only								
Miscellaneous								

Note #1:Home Office, Contractor payments, Depreciated Items and Self-Employed Health Insurance are summarized on dedicated pages a separate section of this book.

Note #2: Track your business miles and vehicle expenses in a separate mileage log to ensure accurate reporting and to determine the best deduction method for your situation.

Note #3: Cost of Goods is in another dedicated section of the book.

Note #4: I suggest you use a payroll program if you have employees that will require issuing a W2 for wages to ensure accurate reporting.

Date								
Vendor or Payee								
Description								Page Total
Advertising								
Commissions & Fees								
Employee Benefit Programs								
Insurance -Other								
Business Interest								
Legal & Professional Services								
Office Expenses								
Pension & Profit Sharing								
Rent or Lease								
Repairs & Maintenance								
Supplies								
Taxes & Licenses								
Travel								
Meals								
Business Utilities Only								
Miscellaneous								

Note #1:Home Office, Contractor payments, Depreciated Items and Self-Employed Health Insurance are summarized on dedicated pages a separate section of this book.

Note #2: Track your business miles and vehicle expenses in a separate mileage log to ensure accurate reporting and to determine the best deduction method for your situation.

Note #3: Cost of Goods is in another dedicated section of the book.

Note #4: I suggest you use a payroll program if you have employees that will require issuing a W2 for wages to ensure accurate reporting.

Date								
Vendor or Payee								
Description								Page Total
Advertising								
Commissions & Fees								
Employee Benefit Programs								
Insurance -Other								
Business Interest								
Legal & Professional Services								
Office Expenses								
Pension & Profit Sharing								
Rent or Lease								
Repairs & Maintenance								
Supplies								
Taxes & Licenses								
Travel								
Meals								
Business Utilities Only								
Miscellaneous								

Note #1:Home Office, Contractor payments, Depreciated Items and Self-Employed Health Insurance are summarized on dedicated pages a separate section of this book.

Note #2: Track your business miles and vehicle expenses in a separate mileage log to ensure accurate reporting and to determine the best deduction method for your situation.

Note #3: Cost of Goods is in another dedicated section of the book.

Note #4: I suggest you use a payroll program if you have employees that will require issuing a W2 for wages to ensure accurate reporting.

Date								
Vendor or Payee								
Description								Page Total
Advertising								
Commissions & Fees								
Employee Benefit Programs								
Insurance -Other								
Business Interest								
Legal & Professional Services								
Office Expenses								
Pension & Profit Sharing								
Rent or Lease								
Repairs & Maintenance								
Supplies								
Taxes & Licenses								
Travel								
Meals								
Business Utilities Only								
Miscellaneous								

Note #1:Home Office, Contractor payments, Depreciated Items and Self-Employed Health Insurance are summarized on dedicated pages a separate section of this book.

Note #2: Track your business miles and vehicle expenses in a separate mileage log to ensure accurate reporting and to determine the best deduction method for your situation.

Note #3: Cost of Goods is in another dedicated section of the book.

Note #4: I suggest you use a payroll program if you have employees that will require issuing a W2 for wages to ensure accurate reporting.

Date								
Vendor or Payee								
Description								Page Total
Advertising								
Commissions & Fees								
Employee Benefit Programs								
Insurance -Other								
Business Interest								
Legal & Professional Services								
Office Expenses								
Pension & Profit Sharing								
Rent or Lease								
Repairs & Maintenance								
Supplies								
Taxes & Licenses								
Travel								
Meals								
Business Utilities Only								
Miscellaneous								

Note #1:Home Office, Contractor payments, Depreciated Items and Self-Employed Health Insurance are summarized on dedicated pages a separate section of this book.

Note #2: Track your business miles and vehicle expenses in a separate mileage log to ensure accurate reporting and to determine the best deduction method for your situation.

Note #3: Cost of Goods is in another dedicated section of the book.

Note #4: I suggest you use a payroll program if you have employees that will require issuing a W2 for wages to ensure accurate reporting.

Date								
Vendor or Payee								
Description								Page Total
Advertising								
Commissions & Fees								
Employee Benefit Programs								
Insurance -Other								
Business Interest								
Legal & Professional Services								
Office Expenses								
Pension & Profit Sharing								
Rent or Lease								
Repairs & Maintenance								
Supplies								
Taxes & Licenses								
Travel								
Meals								
Business Utilities Only								
Miscellaneous								

Note #1:Home Office, Contractor payments, Depreciated Items and Self-Employed Health Insurance are summarized on dedicated pages a separate section of this book.

Note #2: Track your business miles and vehicle expenses in a separate mileage log to ensure accurate reporting and to determine the best deduction method for your situation.

Note #3: Cost of Goods is in another dedicated section of the book.

Note #4: I suggest you use a payroll program if you have employees that will require issuing a W2 for wages to ensure accurate reporting.

Date								
Vendor or Payee								
Description								Page Total
Advertising								
Commissions & Fees								
Employee Benefit Programs								
Insurance -Other								
Business Interest								
Legal & Professional Services								
Office Expenses								
Pension & Profit Sharing								
Rent or Lease								
Repairs & Maintenance								
Supplies								
Taxes & Licenses								
Travel								
Meals								
Business Utilities Only								
Miscellaneous								

Note #1:Home Office, Contractor payments, Depreciated Items and Self-Employed Health Insurance are summarized on dedicated pages a separate section of this book.

Note #2: Track your business miles and vehicle expenses in a separate mileage log to ensure accurate reporting and to determine the best deduction method for your situation.

Note #3: Cost of Goods is in another dedicated section of the book.

Note #4: I suggest you use a payroll program if you have employees that will require issuing a W2 for wages to ensure accurate reporting.

Date								
Vendor or Payee								
Description								Page Total
Advertising								
Commissions & Fees								
Employee Benefit Programs								
Insurance -Other								
Business Interest								
Legal & Professional Services								
Office Expenses								
Pension & Profit Sharing								
Rent or Lease								
Repairs & Maintenance								
Supplies								
Taxes & Licenses								
Travel								
Meals								
Business Utilities Only								
Miscellaneous								

Note #1:Home Office, Contractor payments, Depreciated Items and Self-Employed Health Insurance are summarized on dedicated pages a separate section of this book.

Note #2: Track your business miles and vehicle expenses in a separate mileage log to ensure accurate reporting and to determine the best deduction method for your situation.

Note #3: Cost of Goods is in another dedicated section of the book.

Note #4: I suggest you use a payroll program if you have employees that will require issuing a W2 for wages to ensure accurate reporting.

Date								
Vendor or Payee								
Description								Page Total
Advertising								
Commissions & Fees								
Employee Benefit Programs								
Insurance -Other								
Business Interest								
Legal & Professional Services								
Office Expenses								
Pension & Profit Sharing								
Rent or Lease								
Repairs & Maintenance								
Supplies								
Taxes & Licenses								
Travel								
Meals								
Business Utilities Only								
Miscellaneous								

Note #1:Home Office, Contractor payments, Depreciated Items and Self-Employed Health Insurance are summarized on dedicated pages a separate section of this book.

Note #2: Track your business miles and vehicle expenses in a separate mileage log to ensure accurate reporting and to determine the best deduction method for your situation.

Note #3: Cost of Goods is in another dedicated section of the book.

Note #4: I suggest you use a payroll program if you have employees that will require issuing a W2 for wages to ensure accurate reporting.

Date								
Vendor or Payee								
Description								Page Total
Advertising								
Commissions & Fees								
Employee Benefit Programs								
Insurance -Other								
Business Interest								
Legal & Professional Services								
Office Expenses								
Pension & Profit Sharing								
Rent or Lease								
Repairs & Maintenance								
Supplies								
Taxes & Licenses								
Travel								
Meals								
Business Utilities Only								
Miscellaneous								

Note #1:Home Office, Contractor payments, Depreciated Items and Self-Employed Health Insurance are summarized on dedicated pages a separate section of this book.

Note #2: Track your business miles and vehicle expenses in a separate mileage log to ensure accurate reporting and to determine the best deduction method for your situation.

Note #3: Cost of Goods is in another dedicated section of the book.

Note #4: I suggest you use a payroll program if you have employees that will require issuing a W2 for wages to ensure accurate reporting.

Date								
Vendor or Payee								
Description								Page Total
Advertising								
Commissions & Fees								
Employee Benefit Programs								
Insurance -Other								
Business Interest								
Legal & Professional Services								
Office Expenses								
Pension & Profit Sharing								
Rent or Lease								
Repairs & Maintenance								
Supplies								
Taxes & Licenses								
Travel								
Meals								
Business Utilities Only								
Miscellaneous								

Note #1:Home Office, Contractor payments, Depreciated Items and Self-Employed Health Insurance are summarized on dedicated pages a separate section of this book.

Note #2: Track your business miles and vehicle expenses in a separate mileage log to ensure accurate reporting and to determine the best deduction method for your situation.

Note #3: Cost of Goods is in another dedicated section of the book.

Note #4: I suggest you use a payroll program if you have employees that will require issuing a W2 for wages to ensure accurate reporting.

Date								
Vendor or Payee								
Description								Page Total
Advertising								
Commissions & Fees								
Employee Benefit Programs								
Insurance -Other								
Business Interest								
Legal & Professional Services								
Office Expenses								
Pension & Profit Sharing								
Rent or Lease								
Repairs & Maintenance								
Supplies								
Taxes & Licenses								
Travel								
Meals								
Business Utilities Only								
Miscellaneous								

Note #1:Home Office, Contractor payments, Depreciated Items and Self-Employed Health Insurance are summarized on dedicated pages a separate section of this book.

Note #2: Track your business miles and vehicle expenses in a separate mileage log to ensure accurate reporting and to determine the best deduction method for your situation.

Note #3: Cost of Goods is in another dedicated section of the book.

Note #4: I suggest you use a payroll program if you have employees that will require issuing a W2 for wages to ensure accurate reporting.

Date								
Vendor or Payee								
Description								Page Total
Advertising								
Commissions & Fees								
Employee Benefit Programs								
Insurance -Other								
Business Interest								
Legal & Professional Services								
Office Expenses								
Pension & Profit Sharing								
Rent or Lease								
Repairs & Maintenance								
Supplies								
Taxes & Licenses								
Travel								
Meals								
Business Utilities Only								
Miscellaneous								

Note #1:Home Office, Contractor payments, Depreciated Items and Self-Employed Health Insurance are summarized on dedicated pages a separate section of this book.

Note #2: Track your business miles and vehicle expenses in a separate mileage log to ensure accurate reporting and to determine the best deduction method for your situation.

Note #3: Cost of Goods is in another dedicated section of the book.

Note #4: I suggest you use a payroll program if you have employees that will require issuing a W2 for wages to ensure accurate reporting.

Date								
Vendor or Payee								
Description								Page Total
Advertising								
Commissions & Fees								
Employee Benefit Programs								
Insurance -Other								
Business Interest								
Legal & Professional Services								
Office Expenses								
Pension & Profit Sharing								
Rent or Lease								
Repairs & Maintenance								
Supplies								
Taxes & Licenses								
Travel								
Meals								
Business Utilities Only								
Miscellaneous								

Note #1:Home Office, Contractor payments, Depreciated Items and Self-Employed Health Insurance are summarized on dedicated pages a separate section of this book.

Note #2: Track your business miles and vehicle expenses in a separate mileage log to ensure accurate reporting and to determine the best deduction method for your situation.

Note #3: Cost of Goods is in another dedicated section of the book.

Note #4: I suggest you use a payroll program if you have employees that will require issuing a W2 for wages to ensure accurate reporting.

Date								
Vendor or Payee								
Description								Page Total
Advertising								
Commissions & Fees								
Employee Benefit Programs								
Insurance -Other								
Business Interest								
Legal & Professional Services								
Office Expenses								
Pension & Profit Sharing								
Rent or Lease								
Repairs & Maintenance								
Supplies								
Taxes & Licenses								
Travel								
Meals								
Business Utilities Only								
Miscellaneous								

Note #1:Home Office, Contractor payments, Depreciated Items and Self-Employed Health Insurance are summarized on dedicated pages a separate section of this book.

Note #2: Track your business miles and vehicle expenses in a separate mileage log to ensure accurate reporting and to determine the best deduction method for your situation.

Note #3: Cost of Goods is in another dedicated section of the book.

Note #4: I suggest you use a payroll program if you have employees that will require issuing a W2 for wages to ensure accurate reporting.

Date								
Vendor or Payee								
Description								Page Total
Advertising								
Commissions & Fees								
Employee Benefit Programs								
Insurance -Other								
Business Interest								
Legal & Professional Services								
Office Expenses								
Pension & Profit Sharing								
Rent or Lease								
Repairs & Maintenance								
Supplies								
Taxes & Licenses								
Travel								
Meals								
Business Utilities Only								
Miscellaneous								

Note #1:Home Office, Contractor payments, Depreciated Items and Self-Employed Health Insurance are summarized on dedicated pages a separate section of this book.

Note #2: Track your business miles and vehicle expenses in a separate mileage log to ensure accurate reporting and to determine the best deduction method for your situation.

Note #3: Cost of Goods is in another dedicated section of the book.

Note #4: I suggest you use a payroll program if you have employees that will require issuing a W2 for wages to ensure accurate reporting.

Date								
Vendor or Payee								
Description								Page Total
Advertising								
Commissions & Fees								
Employee Benefit Programs								
Insurance -Other								
Business Interest								
Legal & Professional Services								
Office Expenses								
Pension & Profit Sharing								
Rent or Lease								
Repairs & Maintenance								
Supplies								
Taxes & Licenses								
Travel								
Meals								
Business Utilities Only								
Miscellaneous								

Note #1:Home Office, Contractor payments, Depreciated Items and Self-Employed Health Insurance are summarized on dedicated pages a separate section of this book.

Note #2: Track your business miles and vehicle expenses in a separate mileage log to ensure accurate reporting and to determine the best deduction method for your situation.

Note #3: Cost of Goods is in another dedicated section of the book.

Note #4: I suggest you use a payroll program if you have employees that will require issuing a W2 for wages to ensure accurate reporting.

Date								
Vendor or Payee								
Description								Page Total
Advertising								
Commissions & Fees								
Employee Benefit Programs								
Insurance -Other								
Business Interest								
Legal & Professional Services								
Office Expenses								
Pension & Profit Sharing								
Rent or Lease								
Repairs & Maintenance								
Supplies								
Taxes & Licenses								
Travel								
Meals								
Business Utilities Only								
Miscellaneous								

Note #1:Home Office, Contractor payments, Depreciated Items and Self-Employed Health Insurance are summarized on dedicated pages a separate section of this book.

Note #2: Track your business miles and vehicle expenses in a separate mileage log to ensure accurate reporting and to determine the best deduction method for your situation.

Note #3: Cost of Goods is in another dedicated section of the book.

Note #4: I suggest you use a payroll program if you have employees that will require issuing a W2 for wages to ensure accurate reporting.

Date								
Vendor or Payee								
Description								Page Total
Advertising								
Commissions & Fees								
Employee Benefit Programs								
Insurance -Other								
Business Interest								
Legal & Professional Services								
Office Expenses								
Pension & Profit Sharing								
Rent or Lease								
Repairs & Maintenance								
Supplies								
Taxes & Licenses								
Travel								
Meals								
Business Utilities Only								
Miscellaneous								

Note #1:Home Office, Contractor payments, Depreciated Items and Self-Employed Health Insurance are summarized on dedicated pages a separate section of this book.

Note #2: Track your business miles and vehicle expenses in a separate mileage log to ensure accurate reporting and to determine the best deduction method for your situation.

Note #3: Cost of Goods is in another dedicated section of the book.

Note #4: I suggest you use a payroll program if you have employees that will require issuing a W2 for wages to ensure accurate reporting.

Date								
Vendor or Payee								
Description								Page Total
Advertising								
Commissions & Fees								
Employee Benefit Programs								
Insurance -Other								
Business Interest								
Legal & Professional Services								
Office Expenses								
Pension & Profit Sharing								
Rent or Lease								
Repairs & Maintenance								
Supplies								
Taxes & Licenses								
Travel								
Meals								
Business Utilities Only								
Miscellaneous								

Note #1:Home Office, Contractor payments, Depreciated Items and Self-Employed Health Insurance are summarized on dedicated pages a separate section of this book.

Note #2: Track your business miles and vehicle expenses in a separate mileage log to ensure accurate reporting and to determine the best deduction method for your situation.

Note #3: Cost of Goods is in another dedicated section of the book.

Note #4: I suggest you use a payroll program if you have employees that will require issuing a W2 for wages to ensure accurate reporting.

Date								
Vendor or Payee								
Description								Page Total
Advertising								
Commissions & Fees								
Employee Benefit Programs								
Insurance -Other								
Business Interest								
Legal & Professional Services								
Office Expenses								
Pension & Profit Sharing								
Rent or Lease								
Repairs & Maintenance								
Supplies								
Taxes & Licenses								
Travel								
Meals								
Business Utilities Only								
Miscellaneous								

Note #1:Home Office, Contractor payments, Depreciated Items and Self-Employed Health Insurance are summarized on dedicated pages a separate section of this book.

Note #2: Track your business miles and vehicle expenses in a separate mileage log to ensure accurate reporting and to determine the best deduction method for your situation.

Note #3: Cost of Goods is in another dedicated section of the book.

Note #4: I suggest you use a payroll program if you have employees that will require issuing a W2 for wages to ensure accurate reporting.

Date								
Vendor or Payee								
Description								Page Total
Advertising								
Commissions & Fees								
Employee Benefit Programs								
Insurance -Other								
Business Interest								
Legal & Professional Services								
Office Expenses								
Pension & Profit Sharing								
Rent or Lease								
Repairs & Maintenance								
Supplies								
Taxes & Licenses								
Travel								
Meals								
Business Utilities Only								
Miscellaneous								

Note #1:Home Office, Contractor payments, Depreciated Items and Self-Employed Health Insurance are summarized on dedicated pages a separate section of this book.

Note #2: Track your business miles and vehicle expenses in a separate mileage log to ensure accurate reporting and to determine the best deduction method for your situation.

Note #3: Cost of Goods is in another dedicated section of the book.

Note #4: I suggest you use a payroll program if you have employees that will require issuing a W2 for wages to ensure accurate reporting.

Date								
Vendor or Payee								
Description								Page Total
Advertising								
Commissions & Fees								
Employee Benefit Programs								
Insurance -Other								
Business Interest								
Legal & Professional Services								
Office Expenses								
Pension & Profit Sharing								
Rent or Lease								
Repairs & Maintenance								
Supplies								
Taxes & Licenses								
Travel								
Meals								
Business Utilities Only								
Miscellaneous								

Note #1:Home Office, Contractor payments, Depreciated Items and Self-Employed Health Insurance are summarized on dedicated pages a separate section of this book.

Note #2: Track your business miles and vehicle expenses in a separate mileage log to ensure accurate reporting and to determine the best deduction method for your situation.

Note #3: Cost of Goods is in another dedicated section of the book.

Note #4: I suggest you use a payroll program if you have employees that will require issuing a W2 for wages to ensure accurate reporting.

Date								
Vendor or Payee								
Description								Page Total
Advertising								
Commissions & Fees								
Employee Benefit Programs								
Insurance -Other								
Business Interest								
Legal & Professional Services								
Office Expenses								
Pension & Profit Sharing								
Rent or Lease								
Repairs & Maintenance								
Supplies								
Taxes & Licenses								
Travel								
Meals								
Business Utilities Only								
Miscellaneous								

Note #1:Home Office, Contractor payments, Depreciated Items and Self-Employed Health Insurance are summarized on dedicated pages a separate section of this book.

Note #2: Track your business miles and vehicle expenses in a separate mileage log to ensure accurate reporting and to determine the best deduction method for your situation.

Note #3: Cost of Goods is in another dedicated section of the book.

Note #4: I suggest you use a payroll program if you have employees that will require issuing a W2 for wages to ensure accurate reporting.

Date								
Vendor or Payee								
Description								Page Total
Advertising								
Commissions & Fees								
Employee Benefit Programs								
Insurance -Other								
Business Interest								
Legal & Professional Services								
Office Expenses								
Pension & Profit Sharing								
Rent or Lease								
Repairs & Maintenance								
Supplies								
Taxes & Licenses								
Travel								
Meals								
Business Utilities Only								
Miscellaneous								

Note #1:Home Office, Contractor payments, Depreciated Items and Self-Employed Health Insurance are summarized on dedicated pages a separate section of this book.

Note #2: Track your business miles and vehicle expenses in a separate mileage log to ensure accurate reporting and to determine the best deduction method for your situation.

Note #3: Cost of Goods is in another dedicated section of the book.

Note #4: I suggest you use a payroll program if you have employees that will require issuing a W2 for wages to ensure accurate reporting.

Date								
Vendor or Payee								
Description								Page Total
Advertising								
Commissions & Fees								
Employee Benefit Programs								
Insurance -Other								
Business Interest								
Legal & Professional Services								
Office Expenses								
Pension & Profit Sharing								
Rent or Lease								
Repairs & Maintenance								
Supplies								
Taxes & Licenses								
Travel								
Meals								
Business Utilities Only								
Miscellaneous								

Note #1:Home Office, Contractor payments, Depreciated Items and Self-Employed Health Insurance are summarized on dedicated pages a separate section of this book.

Note #2: Track your business miles and vehicle expenses in a separate mileage log to ensure accurate reporting and to determine the best deduction method for your situation.

Note #3: Cost of Goods is in another dedicated section of the book.

Note #4: I suggest you use a payroll program if you have employees that will require issuing a W2 for wages to ensure accurate reporting.

Date								
Vendor or Payee								
Description								Page Total
Advertising								
Commissions & Fees								
Employee Benefit Programs								
Insurance -Other								
Business Interest								
Legal & Professional Services								
Office Expenses								
Pension & Profit Sharing								
Rent or Lease								
Repairs & Maintenance								
Supplies								
Taxes & Licenses								
Travel								
Meals								
Business Utilities Only								
Miscellaneous								

Note #1:Home Office, Contractor payments, Depreciated Items and Self-Employed Health Insurance are summarized on dedicated pages a separate section of this book.

Note #2: Track your business miles and vehicle expenses in a separate mileage log to ensure accurate reporting and to determine the best deduction method for your situation.

Note #3: Cost of Goods is in another dedicated section of the book.

Note #4: I suggest you use a payroll program if you have employees that will require issuing a W2 for wages to ensure accurate reporting.

Date								
Vendor or Payee								
Description								Page Total
Advertising								
Commissions & Fees								
Employee Benefit Programs								
Insurance -Other								
Business Interest								
Legal & Professional Services								
Office Expenses								
Pension & Profit Sharing								
Rent or Lease								
Repairs & Maintenance								
Supplies								
Taxes & Licenses								
Travel								
Meals								
Business Utilities Only								
Miscellaneous								

Note #1:Home Office, Contractor payments, Depreciated Items and Self-Employed Health Insurance are summarized on dedicated pages a separate section of this book.

Note #2: Track your business miles and vehicle expenses in a separate mileage log to ensure accurate reporting and to determine the best deduction method for your situation.

Note #3: Cost of Goods is in another dedicated section of the book.

Note #4: I suggest you use a payroll program if you have employees that will require issuing a W2 for wages to ensure accurate reporting.

Date								
Vendor or Payee								
Description								Page Total
Advertising								
Commissions & Fees								
Employee Benefit Programs								
Insurance -Other								
Business Interest								
Legal & Professional Services								
Office Expenses								
Pension & Profit Sharing								
Rent or Lease								
Repairs & Maintenance								
Supplies								
Taxes & Licenses								
Travel								
Meals								
Business Utilities Only								
Miscellaneous								

Note #1:Home Office, Contractor payments, Depreciated Items and Self-Employed Health Insurance are summarized on dedicated pages a separate section of this book.

Note #2: Track your business miles and vehicle expenses in a separate mileage log to ensure accurate reporting and to determine the best deduction method for your situation.

Note #3: Cost of Goods is in another dedicated section of the book.

Note #4: I suggest you use a payroll program if you have employees that will require issuing a W2 for wages to ensure accurate reporting.

Date								
Vendor or Payee								
Description								Page Total
Advertising								
Commissions & Fees								
Employee Benefit Programs								
Insurance -Other								
Business Interest								
Legal & Professional Services								
Office Expenses								
Pension & Profit Sharing								
Rent or Lease								
Repairs & Maintenance								
Supplies								
Taxes & Licenses								
Travel								
Meals								
Business Utilities Only								
Miscellaneous								

Note #1:Home Office, Contractor payments, Depreciated Items and Self-Employed Health Insurance are summarized on dedicated pages a separate section of this book.

Note #2: Track your business miles and vehicle expenses in a separate mileage log to ensure accurate reporting and to determine the best deduction method for your situation.

Note #3: Cost of Goods is in another dedicated section of the book.

Note #4: I suggest you use a payroll program if you have employees that will require issuing a W2 for wages to ensure accurate reporting.

Date								
Vendor or Payee								
Description								Page Total
Advertising								
Commissions & Fees								
Employee Benefit Programs								
Insurance -Other								
Business Interest								
Legal & Professional Services								
Office Expenses								
Pension & Profit Sharing								
Rent or Lease								
Repairs & Maintenance								
Supplies								
Taxes & Licenses								
Travel								
Meals								
Business Utilities Only								
Miscellaneous								

Note #1:Home Office, Contractor payments, Depreciated Items and Self-Employed Health Insurance are summarized on dedicated pages a separate section of this book.

Note #2: Track your business miles and vehicle expenses in a separate mileage log to ensure accurate reporting and to determine the best deduction method for your situation.

Note #3: Cost of Goods is in another dedicated section of the book.

Note #4: I suggest you use a payroll program if you have employees that will require issuing a W2 for wages to ensure accurate reporting.

Date								
Vendor or Payee								
Description								Page Total
Advertising								
Commissions & Fees								
Employee Benefit Programs								
Insurance -Other								
Business Interest								
Legal & Professional Services								
Office Expenses								
Pension & Profit Sharing								
Rent or Lease								
Repairs & Maintenance								
Supplies								
Taxes & Licenses								
Travel								
Meals								
Business Utilities Only								
Miscellaneous								

Note #1:Home Office, Contractor payments, Depreciated Items and Self-Employed Health Insurance are summarized on dedicated pages a separate section of this book.

Note #2: Track your business miles and vehicle expenses in a separate mileage log to ensure accurate reporting and to determine the best deduction method for your situation.

Note #3: Cost of Goods is in another dedicated section of the book.

Note #4: I suggest you use a payroll program if you have employees that will require issuing a W2 for wages to ensure accurate reporting.

Date								
Vendor or Payee								
Description								Page Total
Advertising								
Commissions & Fees								
Employee Benefit Programs								
Insurance -Other								
Business Interest								
Legal & Professional Services								
Office Expenses								
Pension & Profit Sharing								
Rent or Lease								
Repairs & Maintenance								
Supplies								
Taxes & Licenses								
Travel								
Meals								
Business Utilities Only								
Miscellaneous								

Note #1:Home Office, Contractor payments, Depreciated Items and Self-Employed Health Insurance are summarized on dedicated pages a separate section of this book.

Note #2: Track your business miles and vehicle expenses in a separate mileage log to ensure accurate reporting and to determine the best deduction method for your situation.

Note #3: Cost of Goods is in another dedicated section of the book.

Note #4: I suggest you use a payroll program if you have employees that will require issuing a W2 for wages to ensure accurate reporting.

Date								
Vendor or Payee								
Description								Page Total
Advertising								
Commissions & Fees								
Employee Benefit Programs								
Insurance -Other								
Business Interest								
Legal & Professional Services								
Office Expenses								
Pension & Profit Sharing								
Rent or Lease								
Repairs & Maintenance								
Supplies								
Taxes & Licenses								
Travel								
Meals								
Business Utilities Only								
Miscellaneous								

Note #1:Home Office, Contractor payments, Depreciated Items and Self-Employed Health Insurance are summarized on dedicated pages a separate section of this book.

Note #2: Track your business miles and vehicle expenses in a separate mileage log to ensure accurate reporting and to determine the best deduction method for your situation.

Note #3: Cost of Goods is in another dedicated section of the book.

Note #4: I suggest you use a payroll program if you have employees that will require issuing a W2 for wages to ensure accurate reporting.

Date								
Vendor or Payee								
Description								Page Total
Advertising								
Commissions & Fees								
Employee Benefit Programs								
Insurance -Other								
Business Interest								
Legal & Professional Services								
Office Expenses								
Pension & Profit Sharing								
Rent or Lease								
Repairs & Maintenance								
Supplies								
Taxes & Licenses								
Travel								
Meals								
Business Utilities Only								
Miscellaneous								

Note #1:Home Office, Contractor payments, Depreciated Items and Self-Employed Health Insurance are summarized on dedicated pages a separate section of this book.

Note #2: Track your business miles and vehicle expenses in a separate mileage log to ensure accurate reporting and to determine the best deduction method for your situation.

Note #3: Cost of Goods is in another dedicated section of the book.

Note #4: I suggest you use a payroll program if you have employees that will require issuing a W2 for wages to ensure accurate reporting.

Date								
Vendor or Payee								
Description								Page Total
Advertising								
Commissions & Fees								
Employee Benefit Programs								
Insurance -Other								
Business Interest								
Legal & Professional Services								
Office Expenses								
Pension & Profit Sharing								
Rent or Lease								
Repairs & Maintenance								
Supplies								
Taxes & Licenses								
Travel								
Meals								
Business Utilities Only								
Miscellaneous								

Note #1:Home Office, Contractor payments, Depreciated Items and Self-Employed Health Insurance are summarized on dedicated pages a separate section of this book.

Note #2: Track your business miles and vehicle expenses in a separate mileage log to ensure accurate reporting and to determine the best deduction method for your situation.

Note #3: Cost of Goods is in another dedicated section of the book.

Note #4: I suggest you use a payroll program if you have employees that will require issuing a W2 for wages to ensure accurate reporting.

Date								
Vendor or Payee								
Description								Page Total
Advertising								
Commissions & Fees								
Employee Benefit Programs								
Insurance -Other								
Business Interest								
Legal & Professional Services								
Office Expenses								
Pension & Profit Sharing								
Rent or Lease								
Repairs & Maintenance								
Supplies								
Taxes & Licenses								
Travel								
Meals								
Business Utilities Only								
Miscellaneous								

Note #1:Home Office, Contractor payments, Depreciated Items and Self-Employed Health Insurance are summarized on dedicated pages a separate section of this book.

Note #2: Track your business miles and vehicle expenses in a separate mileage log to ensure accurate reporting and to determine the best deduction method for your situation.

Note #3: Cost of Goods is in another dedicated section of the book.

Note #4: I suggest you use a payroll program if you have employees that will require issuing a W2 for wages to ensure accurate reporting.

Date								
Vendor or Payee								
Description								Page Total
Advertising								
Commissions & Fees								
Employee Benefit Programs								
Insurance -Other								
Business Interest								
Legal & Professional Services								
Office Expenses								
Pension & Profit Sharing								
Rent or Lease								
Repairs & Maintenance								
Supplies								
Taxes & Licenses								
Travel								
Meals								
Business Utilities Only								
Miscellaneous								

Note #1:Home Office, Contractor payments, Depreciated Items and Self-Employed Health Insurance are summarized on dedicated pages a separate section of this book.

Note #2: Track your business miles and vehicle expenses in a separate mileage log to ensure accurate reporting and to determine the best deduction method for your situation.

Note #3: Cost of Goods is in another dedicated section of the book.

Note #4: I suggest you use a payroll program if you have employees that will require issuing a W2 for wages to ensure accurate reporting.

Date								
Vendor or Payee								
Description								Page Total
Advertising								
Commissions & Fees								
Employee Benefit Programs								
Insurance -Other								
Business Interest								
Legal & Professional Services								
Office Expenses								
Pension & Profit Sharing								
Rent or Lease								
Repairs & Maintenance								
Supplies								
Taxes & Licenses								
Travel								
Meals								
Business Utilities Only								
Miscellaneous								

Note #1:Home Office, Contractor payments, Depreciated Items and Self-Employed Health Insurance are summarized on dedicated pages a separate section of this book.

Note #2: Track your business miles and vehicle expenses in a separate mileage log to ensure accurate reporting and to determine the best deduction method for your situation.

Note #3: Cost of Goods is in another dedicated section of the book.

Note #4: I suggest you use a payroll program if you have employees that will require issuing a W2 for wages to ensure accurate reporting.

Date								
Vendor or Payee								
Description								Page Total
Advertising								
Commissions & Fees								
Employee Benefit Programs								
Insurance -Other								
Business Interest								
Legal & Professional Services								
Office Expenses								
Pension & Profit Sharing								
Rent or Lease								
Repairs & Maintenance								
Supplies								
Taxes & Licenses								
Travel								
Meals								
Business Utilities Only								
Miscellaneous								

Note #1:Home Office, Contractor payments, Depreciated Items and Self-Employed Health Insurance are summarized on dedicated pages a separate section of this book.

Note #2: Track your business miles and vehicle expenses in a separate mileage log to ensure accurate reporting and to determine the best deduction method for your situation.

Note #3: Cost of Goods is in another dedicated section of the book.

Note #4: I suggest you use a payroll program if you have employees that will require issuing a W2 for wages to ensure accurate reporting.

Date								
Vendor or Payee								
Description								Page Total
Advertising								
Commissions & Fees								
Employee Benefit Programs								
Insurance -Other								
Business Interest								
Legal & Professional Services								
Office Expenses								
Pension & Profit Sharing								
Rent or Lease								
Repairs & Maintenance								
Supplies								
Taxes & Licenses								
Travel								
Meals								
Business Utilities Only								
Miscellaneous								

Note #1:Home Office, Contractor payments, Depreciated Items and Self-Employed Health Insurance are summarized on dedicated pages a separate section of this book.

Note #2: Track your business miles and vehicle expenses in a separate mileage log to ensure accurate reporting and to determine the best deduction method for your situation.

Note #3: Cost of Goods is in another dedicated section of the book.

Note #4: I suggest you use a payroll program if you have employees that will require issuing a W2 for wages to ensure accurate reporting.

Date								
Vendor or Payee								
Description								Page Total
Advertising								
Commissions & Fees								
Employee Benefit Programs								
Insurance -Other								
Business Interest								
Legal & Professional Services								
Office Expenses								
Pension & Profit Sharing								
Rent or Lease								
Repairs & Maintenance								
Supplies								
Taxes & Licenses								
Travel								
Meals								
Business Utilities Only								
Miscellaneous								

Note #1:Home Office, Contractor payments, Depreciated Items and Self-Employed Health Insurance are summarized on dedicated pages a separate section of this book.

Note #2: Track your business miles and vehicle expenses in a separate mileage log to ensure accurate reporting and to determine the best deduction method for your situation.

Note #3: Cost of Goods is in another dedicated section of the book.

Note #4: I suggest you use a payroll program if you have employees that will require issuing a W2 for wages to ensure accurate reporting.

Date								
Vendor or Payee								
Description								Page Total
Advertising								
Commissions & Fees								
Employee Benefit Programs								
Insurance -Other								
Business Interest								
Legal & Professional Services								
Office Expenses								
Pension & Profit Sharing								
Rent or Lease								
Repairs & Maintenance								
Supplies								
Taxes & Licenses								
Travel								
Meals								
Business Utilities Only								
Miscellaneous								

Note #1:Home Office, Contractor payments, Depreciated Items and Self-Employed Health Insurance are summarized on dedicated pages a separate section of this book.

Note #2: Track your business miles and vehicle expenses in a separate mileage log to ensure accurate reporting and to determine the best deduction method for your situation.

Note #3: Cost of Goods is in another dedicated section of the book.

Note #4: I suggest you use a payroll program if you have employees that will require issuing a W2 for wages to ensure accurate reporting.

Date								
Vendor or Payee								
Description								Page Total
Advertising								
Commissions & Fees								
Employee Benefit Programs								
Insurance -Other								
Business Interest								
Legal & Professional Services								
Office Expenses								
Pension & Profit Sharing								
Rent or Lease								
Repairs & Maintenance								
Supplies								
Taxes & Licenses								
Travel								
Meals								
Business Utilities Only								
Miscellaneous								

Note #1:Home Office, Contractor payments, Depreciated Items and Self-Employed Health Insurance are summarized on dedicated pages a separate section of this book.

Note #2: Track your business miles and vehicle expenses in a separate mileage log to ensure accurate reporting and to determine the best deduction method for your situation.

Note #3: Cost of Goods is in another dedicated section of the book.

Note #4: I suggest you use a payroll program if you have employees that will require issuing a W2 for wages to ensure accurate reporting.

Date								
Vendor or Payee								
Description								Page Total
Advertising								
Commissions & Fees								
Employee Benefit Programs								
Insurance -Other								
Business Interest								
Legal & Professional Services								
Office Expenses								
Pension & Profit Sharing								
Rent or Lease								
Repairs & Maintenance								
Supplies								
Taxes & Licenses								
Travel								
Meals								
Business Utilities Only								
Miscellaneous								

Note #1:Home Office, Contractor payments, Depreciated Items and Self-Employed Health Insurance are summarized on dedicated pages a separate section of this book.

Note #2: Track your business miles and vehicle expenses in a separate mileage log to ensure accurate reporting and to determine the best deduction method for your situation.

Note #3: Cost of Goods is in another dedicated section of the book.

Note #4: I suggest you use a payroll program if you have employees that will require issuing a W2 for wages to ensure accurate reporting.

Date								
Vendor or Payee								
Description								Page Total
Advertising								
Commissions & Fees								
Employee Benefit Programs								
Insurance -Other								
Business Interest								
Legal & Professional Services								
Office Expenses								
Pension & Profit Sharing								
Rent or Lease								
Repairs & Maintenance								
Supplies								
Taxes & Licenses								
Travel								
Meals								
Business Utilities Only								
Miscellaneous								

Note #1:Home Office, Contractor payments, Depreciated Items and Self-Employed Health Insurance are summarized on dedicated pages a separate section of this book.

Note #2: Track your business miles and vehicle expenses in a separate mileage log to ensure accurate reporting and to determine the best deduction method for your situation.

Note #3: Cost of Goods is in another dedicated section of the book.

Note #4: I suggest you use a payroll program if you have employees that will require issuing a W2 for wages to ensure accurate reporting.

Date								
Vendor or Payee								
Description								Page Total
Advertising								
Commissions & Fees								
Employee Benefit Programs								
Insurance -Other								
Business Interest								
Legal & Professional Services								
Office Expenses								
Pension & Profit Sharing								
Rent or Lease								
Repairs & Maintenance								
Supplies								
Taxes & Licenses								
Travel								
Meals								
Business Utilities Only								
Miscellaneous								

Note #1:Home Office, Contractor payments, Depreciated Items and Self-Employed Health Insurance are summarized on dedicated pages a separate section of this book.

Note #2: Track your business miles and vehicle expenses in a separate mileage log to ensure accurate reporting and to determine the best deduction method for your situation.

Note #3: Cost of Goods is in another dedicated section of the book.

Note #4: I suggest you use a payroll program if you have employees that will require issuing a W2 for wages to ensure accurate reporting.

Date								
Vendor or Payee								
Description								Page Total
Advertising								
Commissions & Fees								
Employee Benefit Programs								
Insurance -Other								
Business Interest								
Legal & Professional Services								
Office Expenses								
Pension & Profit Sharing								
Rent or Lease								
Repairs & Maintenance								
Supplies								
Taxes & Licenses								
Travel								
Meals								
Business Utilities Only								
Miscellaneous								

Note #1:Home Office, Contractor payments, Depreciated Items and Self-Employed Health Insurance are summarized on dedicated pages a separate section of this book.

Note #2: Track your business miles and vehicle expenses in a separate mileage log to ensure accurate reporting and to determine the best deduction method for your situation.

Note #3: Cost of Goods is in another dedicated section of the book.

Note #4: I suggest you use a payroll program if you have employees that will require issuing a W2 for wages to ensure accurate reporting.

Date								
Vendor or Payee								
Description								Page Total
Advertising								
Commissions & Fees								
Employee Benefit Programs								
Insurance -Other								
Business Interest								
Legal & Professional Services								
Office Expenses								
Pension & Profit Sharing								
Rent or Lease								
Repairs & Maintenance								
Supplies								
Taxes & Licenses								
Travel								
Meals								
Business Utilities Only								
Miscellaneous								

Note #1:Home Office, Contractor payments, Depreciated Items and Self-Employed Health Insurance are summarized on dedicated pages a separate section of this book.

Note #2: Track your business miles and vehicle expenses in a separate mileage log to ensure accurate reporting and to determine the best deduction method for your situation.

Note #3: Cost of Goods is in another dedicated section of the book.

Note #4: I suggest you use a payroll program if you have employees that will require issuing a W2 for wages to ensure accurate reporting.

Date								
Vendor or Payee								
Description								Page Total
Advertising								
Commissions & Fees								
Employee Benefit Programs								
Insurance -Other								
Business Interest								
Legal & Professional Services								
Office Expenses								
Pension & Profit Sharing								
Rent or Lease								
Repairs & Maintenance								
Supplies								
Taxes & Licenses								
Travel								
Meals								
Business Utilities Only								
Miscellaneous								

Note #1:Home Office, Contractor payments, Depreciated Items and Self-Employed Health Insurance are summarized on dedicated pages a separate section of this book.

Note #2: Track your business miles and vehicle expenses in a separate mileage log to ensure accurate reporting and to determine the best deduction method for your situation.

Note #3: Cost of Goods is in another dedicated section of the book.

Note #4: I suggest you use a payroll program if you have employees that will require issuing a W2 for wages to ensure accurate reporting.

Date								
Vendor or Payee								
Description								Page Total
Advertising								
Commissions & Fees								
Employee Benefit Programs								
Insurance -Other								
Business Interest								
Legal & Professional Services								
Office Expenses								
Pension & Profit Sharing								
Rent or Lease								
Repairs & Maintenance								
Supplies								
Taxes & Licenses								
Travel								
Meals								
Business Utilities Only								
Miscellaneous								

Note #1:Home Office, Contractor payments, Depreciated Items and Self-Employed Health Insurance are summarized on dedicated pages a separate section of this book.

Note #2: Track your business miles and vehicle expenses in a separate mileage log to ensure accurate reporting and to determine the best deduction method for your situation.

Note #3: Cost of Goods is in another dedicated section of the book.

Note #4: I suggest you use a payroll program if you have employees that will require issuing a W2 for wages to ensure accurate reporting.

Date								
Vendor or Payee								
Description								Page Total
Advertising								
Commissions & Fees								
Employee Benefit Programs								
Insurance -Other								
Business Interest								
Legal & Professional Services								
Office Expenses								
Pension & Profit Sharing								
Rent or Lease								
Repairs & Maintenance								
Supplies								
Taxes & Licenses								
Travel								
Meals								
Business Utilities Only								
Miscellaneous								

Note #1:Home Office, Contractor payments, Depreciated Items and Self-Employed Health Insurance are summarized on dedicated pages a separate section of this book.

Note #2: Track your business miles and vehicle expenses in a separate mileage log to ensure accurate reporting and to determine the best deduction method for your situation.

Note #3: Cost of Goods is in another dedicated section of the book.

Note #4: I suggest you use a payroll program if you have employees that will require issuing a W2 for wages to ensure accurate reporting.

Date								
Vendor or Payee								
Description								Page Total
Advertising								
Commissions & Fees								
Employee Benefit Programs								
Insurance -Other								
Business Interest								
Legal & Professional Services								
Office Expenses								
Pension & Profit Sharing								
Rent or Lease								
Repairs & Maintenance								
Supplies								
Taxes & Licenses								
Travel								
Meals								
Business Utilities Only								
Miscellaneous								

Note #1:Home Office, Contractor payments, Depreciated Items and Self-Employed Health Insurance are summarized on dedicated pages a separate section of this book.

Note #2: Track your business miles and vehicle expenses in a separate mileage log to ensure accurate reporting and to determine the best deduction method for your situation.

Note #3: Cost of Goods is in another dedicated section of the book.

Note #4: I suggest you use a payroll program if you have employees that will require issuing a W2 for wages to ensure accurate reporting.

Date								
Vendor or Payee								
Description								Page Total
Advertising								
Commissions & Fees								
Employee Benefit Programs								
Insurance -Other								
Business Interest								
Legal & Professional Services								
Office Expenses								
Pension & Profit Sharing								
Rent or Lease								
Repairs & Maintenance								
Supplies								
Taxes & Licenses								
Travel								
Meals								
Business Utilities Only								
Miscellaneous								

Note #1:Home Office, Contractor payments, Depreciated Items and Self-Employed Health Insurance are summarized on dedicated pages a separate section of this book.

Note #2: Track your business miles and vehicle expenses in a separate mileage log to ensure accurate reporting and to determine the best deduction method for your situation.

Note #3: Cost of Goods is in another dedicated section of the book.

Note #4: I suggest you use a payroll program if you have employees that will require issuing a W2 for wages to ensure accurate reporting.

Date								
Vendor or Payee								
Description								Page Total
Advertising								
Commissions & Fees								
Employee Benefit Programs								
Insurance -Other								
Business Interest								
Legal & Professional Services								
Office Expenses								
Pension & Profit Sharing								
Rent or Lease								
Repairs & Maintenance								
Supplies								
Taxes & Licenses								
Travel								
Meals								
Business Utilities Only								
Miscellaneous								

Note #1:Home Office, Contractor payments, Depreciated Items and Self-Employed Health Insurance are summarized on dedicated pages a separate section of this book.

Note #2: Track your business miles and vehicle expenses in a separate mileage log to ensure accurate reporting and to determine the best deduction method for your situation.

Note #3: Cost of Goods is in another dedicated section of the book.

Note #4: I suggest you use a payroll program if you have employees that will require issuing a W2 for wages to ensure accurate reporting.

Date								
Vendor or Payee								
Description								Page Total
Advertising								
Commissions & Fees								
Employee Benefit Programs								
Insurance -Other								
Business Interest								
Legal & Professional Services								
Office Expenses								
Pension & Profit Sharing								
Rent or Lease								
Repairs & Maintenance								
Supplies								
Taxes & Licenses								
Travel								
Meals								
Business Utilities Only								
Miscellaneous								

Note #1:Home Office, Contractor payments, Depreciated Items and Self-Employed Health Insurance are summarized on dedicated pages a separate section of this book.

Note #2: Track your business miles and vehicle expenses in a separate mileage log to ensure accurate reporting and to determine the best deduction method for your situation.

Note #3: Cost of Goods is in another dedicated section of the book.

Note #4: I suggest you use a payroll program if you have employees that will require issuing a W2 for wages to ensure accurate reporting.

Date								
Vendor or Payee								
Description								Page Total
Advertising								
Commissions & Fees								
Employee Benefit Programs								
Insurance -Other								
Business Interest								
Legal & Professional Services								
Office Expenses								
Pension & Profit Sharing								
Rent or Lease								
Repairs & Maintenance								
Supplies								
Taxes & Licenses								
Travel								
Meals								
Business Utilities Only								
Miscellaneous								

Note #1:Home Office, Contractor payments, Depreciated Items and Self-Employed Health Insurance are summarized on dedicated pages a separate section of this book.

Note #2: Track your business miles and vehicle expenses in a separate mileage log to ensure accurate reporting and to determine the best deduction method for your situation.

Note #3: Cost of Goods is in another dedicated section of the book.

Note #4: I suggest you use a payroll program if you have employees that will require issuing a W2 for wages to ensure accurate reporting.

Date								
Vendor or Payee								
Description								Page Total
Advertising								
Commissions & Fees								
Employee Benefit Programs								
Insurance -Other								
Business Interest								
Legal & Professional Services								
Office Expenses								
Pension & Profit Sharing								
Rent or Lease								
Repairs & Maintenance								
Supplies								
Taxes & Licenses								
Travel								
Meals								
Business Utilities Only								
Miscellaneous								

Note #1:Home Office, Contractor payments, Depreciated Items and Self-Employed Health Insurance are summarized on dedicated pages a separate section of this book.

Note #2: Track your business miles and vehicle expenses in a separate mileage log to ensure accurate reporting and to determine the best deduction method for your situation.

Note #3: Cost of Goods is in another dedicated section of the book.

Note #4: I suggest you use a payroll program if you have employees that will require issuing a W2 for wages to ensure accurate reporting.

Date								
Vendor or Payee								
Description								Page Total
Advertising								
Commissions & Fees								
Employee Benefit Programs								
Insurance -Other								
Business Interest								
Legal & Professional Services								
Office Expenses								
Pension & Profit Sharing								
Rent or Lease								
Repairs & Maintenance								
Supplies								
Taxes & Licenses								
Travel								
Meals								
Business Utilities Only								
Miscellaneous								

Note #1:Home Office, Contractor payments, Depreciated Items and Self-Employed Health Insurance are summarized on dedicated pages a separate section of this book.

Note #2: Track your business miles and vehicle expenses in a separate mileage log to ensure accurate reporting and to determine the best deduction method for your situation.

Note #3: Cost of Goods is in another dedicated section of the book.

Note #4: I suggest you use a payroll program if you have employees that will require issuing a W2 for wages to ensure accurate reporting.

Date								
Vendor or Payee								
Description								Page Total
Advertising								
Commissions & Fees								
Employee Benefit Programs								
Insurance -Other								
Business Interest								
Legal & Professional Services								
Office Expenses								
Pension & Profit Sharing								
Rent or Lease								
Repairs & Maintenance								
Supplies								
Taxes & Licenses								
Travel								
Meals								
Business Utilities Only								
Miscellaneous								

Note #1:Home Office, Contractor payments, Depreciated Items and Self-Employed Health Insurance are summarized on dedicated pages a separate section of this book.

Note #2: Track your business miles and vehicle expenses in a separate mileage log to ensure accurate reporting and to determine the best deduction method for your situation.

Note #3: Cost of Goods is in another dedicated section of the book.

Note #4: I suggest you use a payroll program if you have employees that will require issuing a W2 for wages to ensure accurate reporting.

Date								
Vendor or Payee								
Description								Page Total
Advertising								
Commissions & Fees								
Employee Benefit Programs								
Insurance -Other								
Business Interest								
Legal & Professional Services								
Office Expenses								
Pension & Profit Sharing								
Rent or Lease								
Repairs & Maintenance								
Supplies								
Taxes & Licenses								
Travel								
Meals								
Business Utilities Only								
Miscellaneous								

Note #1:Home Office, Contractor payments, Depreciated Items and Self-Employed Health Insurance are summarized on dedicated pages a separate section of this book.

Note #2: Track your business miles and vehicle expenses in a separate mileage log to ensure accurate reporting and to determine the best deduction method for your situation.

Note #3: Cost of Goods is in another dedicated section of the book.

Note #4: I suggest you use a payroll program if you have employees that will require issuing a W2 for wages to ensure accurate reporting.

Date								
Vendor or Payee								
Description								Page Total
Advertising								
Commissions & Fees								
Employee Benefit Programs								
Insurance -Other								
Business Interest								
Legal & Professional Services								
Office Expenses								
Pension & Profit Sharing								
Rent or Lease								
Repairs & Maintenance								
Supplies								
Taxes & Licenses								
Travel								
Meals								
Business Utilities Only								
Miscellaneous								

Note #1:Home Office, Contractor payments, Depreciated Items and Self-Employed Health Insurance are summarized on dedicated pages a separate section of this book.

Note #2: Track your business miles and vehicle expenses in a separate mileage log to ensure accurate reporting and to determine the best deduction method for your situation.

Note #3: Cost of Goods is in another dedicated section of the book.

Note #4: I suggest you use a payroll program if you have employees that will require issuing a W2 for wages to ensure accurate reporting.

Date								
Vendor or Payee								
Description								Page Total
Advertising								
Commissions & Fees								
Employee Benefit Programs								
Insurance -Other								
Business Interest								
Legal & Professional Services								
Office Expenses								
Pension & Profit Sharing								
Rent or Lease								
Repairs & Maintenance								
Supplies								
Taxes & Licenses								
Travel								
Meals								
Business Utilities Only								
Miscellaneous								

Note #1:Home Office, Contractor payments, Depreciated Items and Self-Employed Health Insurance are summarized on dedicated pages a separate section of this book.

Note #2: Track your business miles and vehicle expenses in a separate mileage log to ensure accurate reporting and to determine the best deduction method for your situation.

Note #3: Cost of Goods is in another dedicated section of the book.

Note #4: I suggest you use a payroll program if you have employees that will require issuing a W2 for wages to ensure accurate reporting.

Date								
Vendor or Payee								
Description								Page Total
Advertising								
Commissions & Fees								
Employee Benefit Programs								
Insurance -Other								
Business Interest								
Legal & Professional Services								
Office Expenses								
Pension & Profit Sharing								
Rent or Lease								
Repairs & Maintenance								
Supplies								
Taxes & Licenses								
Travel								
Meals								
Business Utilities Only								
Miscellaneous								

Note #1:Home Office, Contractor payments, Depreciated Items and Self-Employed Health Insurance are summarized on dedicated pages a separate section of this book.

Note #2: Track your business miles and vehicle expenses in a separate mileage log to ensure accurate reporting and to determine the best deduction method for your situation.

Note #3: Cost of Goods is in another dedicated section of the book.

Note #4: I suggest you use a payroll program if you have employees that will require issuing a W2 for wages to ensure accurate reporting.

Date								
Vendor or Payee								
Description								Page Total
Advertising								
Commissions & Fees								
Employee Benefit Programs								
Insurance -Other								
Business Interest								
Legal & Professional Services								
Office Expenses								
Pension & Profit Sharing								
Rent or Lease								
Repairs & Maintenance								
Supplies								
Taxes & Licenses								
Travel								
Meals								
Business Utilities Only								
Miscellaneous								

Note #1:Home Office, Contractor payments, Depreciated Items and Self-Employed Health Insurance are summarized on dedicated pages a separate section of this book.

Note #2: Track your business miles and vehicle expenses in a separate mileage log to ensure accurate reporting and to determine the best deduction method for your situation.

Note #3: Cost of Goods is in another dedicated section of the book.

Note #4: I suggest you use a payroll program if you have employees that will require issuing a W2 for wages to ensure accurate reporting.

Date								
Vendor or Payee								
Description								Page Total
Advertising								
Commissions & Fees								
Employee Benefit Programs								
Insurance -Other								
Business Interest								
Legal & Professional Services								
Office Expenses								
Pension & Profit Sharing								
Rent or Lease								
Repairs & Maintenance								
Supplies								
Taxes & Licenses								
Travel								
Meals								
Business Utilities Only								
Miscellaneous								

Note #1:Home Office, Contractor payments, Depreciated Items and Self-Employed Health Insurance are summarized on dedicated pages a separate section of this book.

Note #2: Track your business miles and vehicle expenses in a separate mileage log to ensure accurate reporting and to determine the best deduction method for your situation.

Note #3: Cost of Goods is in another dedicated section of the book.

Note #4: I suggest you use a payroll program if you have employees that will require issuing a W2 for wages to ensure accurate reporting.

Date								
Vendor or Payee								
Description								Page Total
Advertising								
Commissions & Fees								
Employee Benefit Programs								
Insurance -Other								
Business Interest								
Legal & Professional Services								
Office Expenses								
Pension & Profit Sharing								
Rent or Lease								
Repairs & Maintenance								
Supplies								
Taxes & Licenses								
Travel								
Meals								
Business Utilities Only								
Miscellaneous								

Note #1:Home Office, Contractor payments, Depreciated Items and Self-Employed Health Insurance are summarized on dedicated pages a separate section of this book.

Note #2: Track your business miles and vehicle expenses in a separate mileage log to ensure accurate reporting and to determine the best deduction method for your situation.

Note #3: Cost of Goods is in another dedicated section of the book.

Note #4: I suggest you use a payroll program if you have employees that will require issuing a W2 for wages to ensure accurate reporting.

Date								
Vendor or Payee								
Description								Page Total
Advertising								
Commissions & Fees								
Employee Benefit Programs								
Insurance -Other								
Business Interest								
Legal & Professional Services								
Office Expenses								
Pension & Profit Sharing								
Rent or Lease								
Repairs & Maintenance								
Supplies								
Taxes & Licenses								
Travel								
Meals								
Business Utilities Only								
Miscellaneous								

Note #1:Home Office, Contractor payments, Depreciated Items and Self-Employed Health Insurance are summarized on dedicated pages a separate section of this book.

Note #2: Track your business miles and vehicle expenses in a separate mileage log to ensure accurate reporting and to determine the best deduction method for your situation.

Note #3: Cost of Goods is in another dedicated section of the book.

Note #4: I suggest you use a payroll program if you have employees that will require issuing a W2 for wages to ensure accurate reporting.

MONTHLY CLOSEOUT MINI-CHECKLIST

(This is how freelancers and independent contractors avoid a year-end meltdown.)

If you do nothing else, do this once a month. It takes 20–30 minutes and saves hours later.

Monthly Closeout (Freelancers & Independent Contractors)

✓ Download or save monthly statements for business accounts/credit cards (or export transactions)
✓ Save monthly payment processor summaries if you accept card payments (Stripe/PayPal/Square/etc.)
✓ Complete the Monthly Deposit Reconciliation page (invoices/gross received → fees/refunds → net deposits)
✓ Update the Invoice & Payment Tracker (who paid, who didn't, follow-up dates)
✓ Update the Subscriptions & Software Tracker (new tools, renewals, cancellations)
✓ Update Client Project Costs & Reimbursables (job costs, reimbursables billed/paid)
✓ Add business-purpose notes for any ambiguous charges ("Amazon," "Office Depot," "Misc.")
✓ Save receipts/support for any major purchases (equipment, travel, large professional invoices)

Optional but smart

✓ Quick subscription audit: cancel what you don't use
✓ Review year-to-date totals by category (catch missing expenses while it's easy)
✓ Review mixed-use percentages quarterly (phone/internet/vehicle/home office) and document any changes

WORKSHEET: MONTHLY CLOSEOUT TRACKER

Month	Reports Saved (Y/N)	Deposits Reconciled (Y/N)	Subs Updated (Y/N)	Brand Deals Logged (Y/N)	Affiliate Updated (Y/N)	Notes
Jan						
Feb						
Mar						
Apr						
May						
Jun						
Jul						
Aug						
Sep						
Oct						
Nov						
Dec						

Annual Home Office Worksheets Section

Use Office Space #1 and Office Space #2 (Especially If You Move Mid-Year)

Freelancers and independent contractors don't always work from the same place all year. You might:

- **move during the year**
- **change your primary work area from one room to another**
- **temporarily work from a different home**
- **rent a coworking space or private office for part of the year**
- **shift from "kitchen table mode" to a dedicated workspace mid-year**

That's exactly why this edition includes two home office worksheets.

How to Use Office Space #1 and Office Space #2

- **Use Office Space #1 for your primary home office setup.**
- **Use Office Space #2 if you:**
    - **moved during the year, or**
    - **changed your primary workspace location, or**
    - **started the year in one home office and ended in another.**

What Matters Most for Home Office Tracking

- **Your workspace should be used regularly for business.**
- **Keep your records consistent.**
- **Save simple proof when helpful:**
    - **a photo of the workspace**
    - **a quick sketch with measurements**
    - **a note of the date you moved or changed rooms**
    - **a short explanation of how the space is used for your business**

Don't Overcomplicate It

The goal is not to win a math contest. The goal is to keep clear, reasonable, consistent records that match real life.

Practical Tip (Not Perfect)

If your "home office" is a shared room or mixed-use space, document business use carefully and stay conservative. If you're not sure how your situation fits the rules, ask your tax professional. The worksheet still helps you gather the facts clearly.

Annual Home Office Worksheet for Office Space #1

Annual Home Office Worksheet for Office Space #2

Date office placed in service: ______________________

Date Office removed from service: ______________________

Office Square Footage: ______________________

Total Home Square Footage: ______________________

Home Office Type (Check One Reporting Method): Regular Simplified

If used for daycare:

Days used per year: ________ **Hours per day:** __________

Expenses (Check whether Whole Property or Office Only):

Mortgage Interest: Whole Property ☐ Office Only ☐ **Amount:** ________

Real Estate Taxes: Whole property ☐ Office Only ☐ **Amount:** ________

Insurance: Whole property ☐ Office Only ☐ **Amount:** ________

Rent: Whole property ☐ Office Only ☐ **Amount:** ________

Repairs & Maintenance: Whole property ☐ Office Only ☐ **Amount:** ________

Utilities – Electric: **Amount:** ________

Utilities – Gas: **Amount:** ________

Utilities: Fuel Oil **Amount:** ________

Utilities: Propane **Amount:** ________

Utilities – Water: **Amount:** ________

Utilities – Trash: **Amount:** ________

Utilities – Alarm: **Amount:** ________

Utilities – Phone: **Amount:** _______

Utilities – Internet: **Amount:** _______

Utilities – Cable: **Amount:** _______

Other Costs:

HOA Fees: ______________________________

Condominium Fees: ______________________________

Landscaping/Mowing: ______________________________

Cleaning Services: ______________________________

Pest Control: ______________________________

Home's Adjusted Basis: ______________________________

Home's Fair Market Value: ______________________________

Land Value: ______________________________

Purchase Date: ______________________________

Date Placed in Service: ______________________________

Carryover Losses from Prior tax return year _______ form 8829 Line 43: _______

Carryover Losses from Prior tax return year _______form 8829 Line 44: _______

Annual Home Office Worksheet for Office Space #2

Date office placed in service: ______________________

Date Office removed from service: ______________________

Office Square Footage: ______________________

Total Home Square Footage: ______________________

Home Office Type (Check One Reporting Method): Regular ☐ Simplified ☐

If used for daycare:

Days used per year: ________ **Hours per day:** ________

Expenses (Check whether Whole Property or Office Only):

Mortgage Interest: Whole Property ☐ Office Only ☐ **Amount:** ________

Real Estate Taxes: Whole property ☐ Office Only ☐ **Amount:** ________

Insurance: Whole property ☐ Office Only ☐ **Amount:** ________

Rent: Whole property ☐ Office Only ☐ **Amount:** ________

Repairs & Maintenance: Whole property ☐ Office Only ☐ **Amount:** ________

Utilities – Electric: **Amount:** ________

Utilities – Gas: **Amount:** ________

Utilities: Fuel Oil **Amount:**________

Utilities: Propane **Amount:**________

Utilities – Water: **Amount:** ________

Utilities – Trash: **Amount:** ________

Utilities – Alarm: **Amount:** ________

Utilities – Phone: **Amount:** ________

Utilities – Internet: **Amount:** ________

Utilities – Cable: **Amount:** ________

Other Costs:

HOA Fees: ______________________________

Condominium Fees: ______________________________

Landscaping/Mowing: ______________________________

Cleaning Services: ______________________________

Pest Control: ______________________________

Home's Adjusted Basis: ______________________________

Home's Fair Market Value: ______________________________

Land Value: ______________________________

Purchase Date: ______________________________

Date Placed in Service: ______________________________

Carryover Losses from Prior tax return year ________ form 8829 Line 43: ________

Carryover Losses from Prior tax return year ________form 8829 Line 44: ________

Annual Self-Employed Health Insurance Worksheet

Ineligible Premiums:

- Employer-sponsored group plan coverage

- Amounts paid with pre-tax dollars

Medical Insurance Premiums: ______________________________

Dental Insurance Premiums: ______________________________

Vision Insurance Premiums: ______________________________

Medicare Part B Premiums: ______________________________

Medicare Part D Premiums: ______________________________

Medigap Premiums: ______________________________

Supplemental coverage: ______________________________

Long-Term Care Premiums Spouse name ______________________(Limits apply):$_________

Long-Term Care Premiums Spouse name ______________________(Limits apply):$_________

Cancer/Specified Disease Premiums: ______________________________

Air Ambulance Coverage Premiums: ______________________________

Notes:

WHEN YOU HIRE HELP

(Subcontractors & Independent Contractors)

Who counts, what to track, and how to use the contractor logs in this book

As a freelancer or independent contractor, you may hire help sooner than you expect—especially when work ramps up or a project needs skills you don't want to do yourself.

Common examples of outsourced help:

- **virtual assistant / admin support**
- **bookkeeping**
- **graphic design (proposals, branding, client materials)**
- **web updates / tech support**
- **copyediting / proofreading**
- **subcontractors who help deliver a client project**
- **specialized consultants (project-based support)**

If you pay a person or business for work that supports your freelance/contract work, you want a clean record.

Who Counts as "Hired Help" (Plain English)

In general, hired help is someone who:

- **is not your employee, and**
- **you pay to do work for your business, and**
- **they control how they do the work (they're not under day-to-day direction like an employee).**

You don't have to label everything perfectly all year. You just need to track payments and collect the right info early so year-end doesn't become chaos.

What to Collect at the Start (Before You Pay, Ideally)

- Name / business name
- Mailing address
- Email
- Tax form (often Form W-9 for U.S. contractors)

Where to Log These Payments in This Book

Use the contractor tracking pages to record:

- contractor name and contact info
- date(s) paid
- amount(s) paid
- payment method
- whether you have a W-9 on file
- what the work was for (short description)

Simple rule that protects you:
If you won't remember what you paid them for six months from now, write it down today.
Examples: "VA admin," "Bookkeeping cleanup," "Website updates," "Design for proposal template," "Subcontractor support — Client X project."

Important Note (Evergreen)

Rules and thresholds for information reporting (like 1099 requirements) can change. Track payments cleanly all year, then confirm the current year's reporting requirements with your tax professional or current IRS guidance.

Contract Labor Records for Preparing 1099s

W-9 vs. W-8BEN and When 1099s May Be Required

Freelancers and independent contractors often hire help—sometimes regularly, sometimes only when a project demands it. You may outsource:

- virtual assistant/admin support
- bookkeeping
- graphic design
- web updates/tech support
- subcontractors who help deliver client work
- other specialized services tied to your business

If you pay people who are not your employees, one habit keeps year-end clean:

Collect the right tax form before (or as soon as) you start paying them.

W-9: For U.S. contractors and U.S. businesses

When you pay a non-employee worker and they are a U.S. person or U.S. entity (U.S. citizen, resident alien, or U.S. business), request Form W-9.

The W-9 provides the payees:

- correct legal name
- address
- taxpayer identification number (TIN)

That's the information you need to determine whether a 1099 is required and to prepare it correctly if it is.

W-8BEN (or other W-8 forms): For foreign contractors

If the payee is a foreign person or foreign entity under U.S. tax rules, you generally use Form W-8BEN (or another W-8 form depending on the situation). This certifies foreign status and supports the correct tax treatment and any withholding rules that may apply.

International payments can get technical quickly. Keep the form on file and coordinate with a qualified tax professional if you hire outside the U.S.

When 1099s May Be Required (General Guidance)

In general, if you pay non-employee contractors in the course of your business, you may be required to issue a 1099 (commonly Form 1099-NEC, and sometimes 1099-MISC depending on the payment type). These forms are provided to the payee and filed with the IRS early in the following year.

Important: Rules and thresholds for 1099 reporting can change. Instead of relying on a specific dollar amount printed in a book, use this approach:

- Track contractor payments throughout the year
- Keep W-9s (or W-8 forms) on file
- Confirm the current-year 1099 rules with your tax professional or current IRS guidance before issuing forms

This workbook's contractor tracking pages are here to make that process simple: who you paid, how much, when, how, and what the work was for—so year-end reporting (if required) is fast and accurate.

W-2 Employee Wages Are Not Tracked in This Workbook

This workbook is designed for freelancer/independent contractor recordkeeping. If you have employees, do not try to track payroll manually in a logbook.

For proper compliance, use a qualified payroll service or payroll software to manage:

- paychecks and withholdings
- quarterly payroll filings
- year-end W-2/W-3 reporting

This workbook can still support your business records, but employee payroll must be managed through a payroll system.

If you paid someone for a specific client project, also log that payment in the Client Project Costs tracker so you can see true project profitability.

Contractor #1

Name:____

Address:______________________________________

Address:______________________________________

Address:______________________________________

Form on file: W-9 (U.S.) or W-8BEN (Foreign) ***(circle one)***

Date paid__________________ **Amount $**________________

Date paid__________________ **Amount $**________________

Date paid__________________ **Amount $**________________

Date paid__________________ **Amount $**________________

Date paid__________________ **Amount $**________________

Date paid__________________ **Amount $**________________

Date paid__________________ **Amount $**________________

Date paid__________________ **Amount $**________________

Date paid__________________ **Amount $**________________

Date paid__________________ **Amount $**________________

Date paid__________________ **Amount $**________________

Date paid__________________ **Amount $**________________

Date paid__________________ **Amount $**________________

Date paid__________________ **Amount $**________________

Date paid__________________ **Amount $**________________

Date paid__________________ **Amount $**________________

Date paid__________________ **Amount $**________________

Date paid__________________ **Amount $**________________

Date paid__________________ **Amount $**________________

Total **$**________________

Contractor #2

Name:____

Address:____

Address:____

Address:____

Form on file: W-9 (U.S.) or W-8BEN (Foreign) *(circle one)*

Date paid____________________ Amount $_________________

Date paid____________________ Amount $_________________

Date paid____________________ Amount $_________________

Date paid____________________ Amount $_________________

Date paid____________________ Amount $_________________

Date paid____________________ Amount $_________________

Date paid____________________ Amount $_________________

Date paid____________________ Amount $_________________

Date paid____________________ Amount $_________________

Date paid____________________ Amount $_________________

Date paid____________________ Amount $_________________

Date paid____________________ Amount $_________________

Date paid____________________ Amount $_________________

Date paid____________________ Amount $_________________

Date paid____________________ Amount $_________________

Date paid____________________ Amount $_________________

Date paid____________________ Amount $_________________

Date paid____________________ Amount $_________________

Date paid____________________ Amount $_________________

Total $_________________

Contractor #3

Name:____

Address:______________________________________

Address:______________________________________

Address:______________________________________

Form on file: W-9 (U.S.) or W-8BEN (Foreign) ***(circle one)***

Date paid__________________ **Amount $**_______________

Date paid__________________ **Amount $**_______________

Date paid__________________ **Amount $**_______________

Date paid__________________ **Amount $**_______________

Date paid__________________ **Amount $**_______________

Date paid__________________ **Amount $**_______________

Date paid__________________ **Amount $**_______________

Date paid__________________ **Amount $**_______________

Date paid__________________ **Amount $**_______________

Date paid__________________ **Amount $**_______________

Date paid__________________ **Amount $**_______________

Date paid__________________ **Amount $**_______________

Date paid__________________ **Amount $**_______________

Date paid__________________ **Amount $**_______________

Date paid__________________ **Amount $**_______________

Date paid__________________ **Amount $**_______________

Date paid__________________ **Amount $**_______________

Date paid__________________ **Amount $**_______________

Date paid__________________ **Amount $**_______________

Total **$**_______________

Contractor #4

Name:____

Address:______________________________________

Address:______________________________________

Address:______________________________________

Form on file: W-9 (U.S.) or W-8BEN (Foreign) *(circle one)*

Date paid__________________ **Amount $**_______________

Date paid__________________ **Amount $**_______________

Date paid__________________ **Amount $**_______________

Date paid__________________ **Amount $**_______________

Date paid__________________ **Amount $**_______________

Date paid__________________ **Amount $**_______________

Date paid__________________ **Amount $**_______________

Date paid__________________ **Amount $**_______________

Date paid__________________ **Amount $**_______________

Date paid__________________ **Amount $**_______________

Date paid__________________ **Amount $**_______________

Date paid__________________ **Amount $**_______________

Date paid__________________ **Amount $**_______________

Date paid__________________ **Amount $**_______________

Date paid__________________ **Amount $**_______________

Date paid__________________ **Amount $**_______________

Date paid__________________ **Amount $**_______________

Date paid__________________ **Amount $**_______________

Date paid__________________ **Amount $**_______________

Total **$**_______________

Contractor #5

Name:____

Address:______________________________________

Address:______________________________________

Address:______________________________________

Form on file: W-9 (U.S.) or W-8BEN (Foreign) ***(circle one)***

Date paid__________________ **Amount $**_______________

Date paid__________________ **Amount $**_______________

Date paid__________________ **Amount $**_______________

Date paid__________________ **Amount $**_______________

Date paid__________________ **Amount $**_______________

Date paid__________________ **Amount $**_______________

Date paid__________________ **Amount $**_______________

Date paid__________________ **Amount $**_______________

Date paid__________________ **Amount $**_______________

Date paid__________________ **Amount $**_______________

Date paid__________________ **Amount $**_______________

Date paid__________________ **Amount $**_______________

Date paid__________________ **Amount $**_______________

Date paid__________________ **Amount $**_______________

Date paid__________________ **Amount $**_______________

Date paid__________________ **Amount $**_______________

Date paid__________________ **Amount $**_______________

Date paid__________________ **Amount $**_______________

Date paid__________________ **Amount $**_______________

Total **$**_______________

PROJECT PROFIT SNAPSHOT

This worksheet helps you track:

- **what you earned**
- **what you spent to deliver the job**
- **what you outsourced**
- **what you actually kept**

Use it for:

- **fixed-fee client projects**
- **retainers**
- **milestone-based contracts**
- **onsite assignments**
- **any job that "should have been profitable" but didn't feel like it**

This is not a tax form. It's a business decision tool so you price better and choose better projects.

WORKSHEET: PROJECT PROFIT SNAPSHOT

Project/Job Name: ______________________

Client: ______________________________

Dates: //____ to //____

Service Type: ☐ Hourly ☐ Flat Fee ☐ Retainer ☐ Milestones ☐ Other: ________

Payment Method/Source (optional): ________________________

Income (Project-Related)

Income Type **Amount Date Received Notes**

Deposit / Retainer received

Milestone payment(s)

Final payment

Reimbursables billed to client (if applicable)

Other

Total Project Income: $__________

Expenses (Project-Specific Only)

Only list costs you incurred because of this job.

Expense

Amount

Date

Notes

Subcontractor / outsourced help

Expense

Travel / mileage / parking / tolls

Software/tools purchased specifically for this job

Printing / shipping / courier (client deliverables)

Stock licenses/materials required for delivery

Meeting room / coworking day pass (for client meeting)

Other

Total Project Expenses: $__________

Net Profit Snapshot (The Part People Avoid)

Net (before taxes): Total Income – Total Expenses = $__________

Time (Optional but Eye-Opening)

Estimated hours spent: ______

If you want: Effective hourly rate estimate
(Total Income – Total Expenses) ÷ Hours = $________/hr.

You don't need this for taxes. You need it for pricing, boundaries, and deciding whether you would take this job again if offered or available.

Project Notes (The Truth)

What worked? What didn't? Would you do this type of job again—and under what terms?

____

____

____

____

EQUIPMENT AND ASSET LOG

(Part 1 — What belongs here and why)

Freelancers and independent contractors buy "stuff" to run the business. The tax world often calls higher-cost, longer-life items assets.

This section exists because bigger purchases don't behave like normal supplies. You want a clean list of:

- **what you bought**
- **when you bought it**
- **what it's used for**
- **whether it's mainly business, mainly personal, or mixed-use**

Your tax professional will oversee final classification. Your job is to track what happened.

Examples of equipment/assets that belong in an Asset Log

- **laptop/desktop computer, monitor(s)**
- **tablet used for business work**
- **phone used primarily for business**
- **printer/scanner and office equipment**
- **external hard drives / backup devices**
- **specialized tools required to deliver your services**
- **paid software "lifetime licenses" or major one-time tech purchases**
- **furniture/equipment for a dedicated workspace (where applicable)**

Repairs vs. supplies vs. assets (keep it simple)

- **Repairs often go under repairs/maintenance (fixing what you already own).**
- **Small accessories (cables, adapters, ink, small add-ons) are typically supplies.**
- **Bigger items with longer useful life belong here in the Asset Log.**

Don't overthink it. Track it. Let the tax pro classify it.

Mixed-use is normal

A computer used for both personal and business? Normal.

A phone used for everything? Also ,normal.

The key is being consistent and reasonable about your business-use percentage and keeping a short note that explains your method.

WORKSHEET: FREELANCER GEAR & EQUIPMENT LOG

(Track purchases all year. One line per item.)

Tax Year: __________ Freelancer Brand: ___________________________

Date Purchased	Item / Description	Vendor Cost	Payment Method	Business Use %	Primary Use (filming / editing / audio/ etc.)	Notes (serial #, warranty, reason for purchase)

Assets to Review With Your Tax Pro

This page is your "don't forget this later" list.

Some purchases may need special handling at tax time (for example: depreciation, expensing elections, mixed-use considerations, or business-use documentation). You do not need to decide the tax treatment here.

Your job: capture the facts clearly so you and your tax pro can decide the right treatment quickly.

When to Add Something to This List

Add an item here if it meets any of these:

- **It was a larger purchase (set your own threshold): $________ or more**
- **It will be used for more than one year**
- **It is partly business and partly personal (mixed-use)**
- **It replaced/upgraded something significant**
- **You aren't sure whether it's a supply vs. an asset**
- **It was financed or bought with a payment plan**

Depreciation list of Items

WORKSHEET: Assets to Review With Your Tax Pro (The Usual)

Tax Year: __________ Business Name (if any): ____________________________

Date Purchased	Item / Description	Cost Vendor	Paid in Full? (Y/N)	If Financed Lender / Plan	Business Use %	Why it Matters						Notes (serial #, upgrade, disposed old item, etc.)
						Large	Purchase	Mixed-use	Upgrade	Unsure	Financed	

Year-End Reminder (So This Page Does Its Job)

Before tax preparation:

- ☐ Compare this list to your bank/credit card statements (catch missing items)
- ☐ Confirm business-use percentages are reasonable and consistent
- ☐ Note if any item was sold, traded in, lost, or disposed of during the year

Optional (helpful): keep receipts, invoices, and warranty/serial info with your tax records.

COST OF GOODS SOLD (COGS) — ONLY IF APPLICABLE

This page is only for freelancers/independent contractors who sell physical products and maintain inventory (even small inventory). Examples: selling printed products, physical kits, retail items, or products you purchase/make and resell.

If you provide services only and do not sell physical products, skip this page.

Important: COGS rules can be technical. Timing and classification matter. This section is intentionally brief. If you're unsure how to use it—especially if you also record related expenses elsewhere—confirm the correct treatment with a qualified tax professional.

Method used to value closing inventory (circle one):

Cost Lower of Cost or Market Other (explain): ________________

WORKSHEET: COST OF GOODS SOLD (COGS) SUMMARY

Inventory at the beginning of the year: $_______________

Purchases (items bought to resell / materials that become the product): $_______________

Items withdrawn for personal use: $_______________

Cost of labor (do not include amounts paid to yourself): $_______________

Materials and supplies (used to make/prepare products): $_______________

Other costs (explain): _______________ ______________________ $_______________

Inventory at the end of the year: $_______________

Quick Notes (Keep It Clean)

- **COGS is for product costs (what it costs you to produce/purchase what you sell).**
- **Your time is not COGS. Don't include payments to yourself.**
- **If you're not tracking inventory at all, you may not need this page.**

Merchandise & Physical Product (COGS) — only if applicable

Item	Date of Purchase	Date placed in Service	Cost	% of business use

DIGITAL PRODUCTS (OPTIONAL) — TRACKER

Use this page only if you sell digital products as part of your independent business (templates, downloads, client toolkits, mini trainings, etc.).

Digital product income is easy to mis-track because deposits often come through platforms that deduct fees, issue refunds, or bundle payments.

Tip: If your digital product is a major income stream, track it separately like a mini business inside your business. That's how you spot profit leaks.

WORKSHEET: DIGITAL PRODUCT INVENTORY LIST

Tax Year: __________ **Freelancer Brand:** ____

Product Name	Type (template/course/etc.)	Platform(s) Sold On	Launch Date	Price	Notes

WORKSHEET: DIGITAL PRODUCT MONTHLY SUMMARY

(Use one per month, or one per product—your choice.)

Month: ___________________

Product	Gross Sales	Platform/ Processing Fees	Refunds/ Chargebacks	Contractor Costs	Net Received	Notes

CLIENT SALES TAXES (Rare but Possible)

Most freelancers and independent contractors sell services, not physical products. In many places, services are not subject to sales tax.

But "not usually" is different from "never."

Some states (and some local jurisdictions) tax certain types of services, and rules can vary based on:

- what service do you provide
- where the client is located
- where you perform the work
- whether the service is delivered electronically or in person
- whether you bundle services with taxable items

This page is here for one reason: so, you don't get surprised.

When Sales Tax on Services Might Apply

Sales tax on services is more likely to come up if you:

- collaborate with clients in multiple states
- provide a service category that some states treat as taxable
- sell packages that include both services and taxable items
- invoice for service + tangible deliverables (printed materials, physical items)
- operate locally in a jurisdiction that taxes certain services

You don't have to memorize the rules. You just need a way to flag the issue when it appears.

The One Smart Habit

Track where your clients are and what you sell them.

If a question ever comes up, clean records save time and reduce risk.

WORKSHEET: CLIENT SERVICE SALES TAX CHECK (IF APPLICABLE)

Tax Year: _________ Business Name (if any): _________________________

Client / Project	Client Location (State)	Service Type (Short)	Delivered Where? (Your State / Client State / Remote)	Bundles with Any Taxable Items? (Y/N)	Sales Tax Charged? (Y/N)	Notes / Proof Saved

Notes / Proof Saved examples:

- **"Checked state guidance on taxable services"**
- **"CPA confirmed not taxable for this service"**
- **"Invoice shows separate line items for service vs deliverables"**

Practical Guidance (Keep It Simple)

- **If you're service-only, this may never apply.**
- **If you sell across state lines and you're unsure, ask a qualified professional before you start charging (or not charging) tax.**
- **Rules change. Don't rely on what someone "heard" online.**

Bottom line: This page isn't here to make you anxious. It's here to make you organized if the issue ever shows up.

MONTHLY TAX SET-ASIDE PLANNER

Part 1 — The simple method that keeps you out of trouble

Freelancers and independent contractors don't usually get behind on taxes because they're irresponsible.

They get behind because income is uneven, fees can be deducted before deposits hit the bank, and nobody is withholding taxes for you like a W-2 job.

Here's a simple system that works without turning your life into a spreadsheet museum:

The "Set-Aside" Method (simple + reliable)

Every time money comes in, you immediately set aside a percentage for taxes.
Not later. Not "when you remember." Immediately.

Step 1: Pick your set-aside percentage

This is a planning tool, not a legal promise. Your real number depends on profit level, deductions, and where you live.

A practical starting range many freelancers use:

- **25% = lower profit, heavier expenses, or you're rebuilding/starting out**
- **30% = common "safe default" for many freelancers**
- **35% = higher profit, fewer expenses, stronger safety margin**
- **40% = very profitable year, or you want to be extra conservative**

If you're not sure, start higher and adjust later. It's easier to refund yourself than to come up short.

Step 2: Use the right "base" for the set-aside

Freelancer income can arrive through invoices, ACH, checks, and processors. For your set-aside calculation, use a base that is real and trackable:

☐ **Net deposits (what hit your bank) — recommended for simplicity**
☐ **Gross payments received (before processing fees) — also valid if tracked consistently**

Pick one and stick with it.

Step 3: Move the money out of your spending account

Best practice: put tax set-aside money into a separate account labeled TAX HOLD (or a dedicated savings "bucket") so you don't accidentally spend it.

Step 4: Review quarterly

Quarterly reviews keep you from being surprised. If income or expenses change, adjust your set-aside percentage.

WORKSHEET: TAX SET-ASIDE SETTINGS

Tax Year: _________ Business Name (if any): ______________________________________

My set-aside percentage: _____%

I calculate set-aside using:
☐ Net deposits (recommended) ☐ Gross payments received

Where tax money goes:
☐ Separate account ☐ Separate savings "bucket" ☐ Other: _______________________

Why I chose this percentage (quick note):

____

____

My "Do this every time I get paid" rule:
☐ Transfer _____% of each payment/deposit into TAX HOLD within 24–48 hours.

____

____

(Part 2 — Track deposits, set-aside, and quarterly review)

This page is where the plan becomes real.

You don't need perfect accuracy every week. You need a system that holds up all year.

WORKSHEET: MONTHLY SET-ASIDE TRACKER

(Use one per month.)

Month: ____________________

Date	Deposit Source (platform / processor)	Net Deposit Amount	Set-aside %	Tax-Set-Aside Amount	Moved to TAX HOLD? (Y/N)	Notes

Month totals:

Total net deposits: $___________

Total set-aside moved: $___________

QUARTERLY TAX SET-ASIDE PLANNER

Part 2 — Track deposits, set-aside, and quarterly review

This page is where the plan becomes real.

You don't need perfect accuracy every week. You need a system that holds up all year.

(Use this at the end of each quarter.)

Quarter	Total Net Deposits	Total Set-Aside Saved	Any big changes? (income / expenses)	Adjust my %? (Y/N)	New %
Q1					
Q2					
Q3					
Q4					

Big changes I should tell my tax pro about

☐ Income jumped (new major client / large contract / more work volume)
☐ I added a new service line or changed pricing significantly
☐ I started taking more payments through processors (fees/chargebacks increased)
☐ I traveled heavily for client work
☐ I bought major equipment (computer, office equipment, specialized tools)
☐ I hired subcontractors or outsourced significant work
☐ I moved or changed my work location mid-year
☐ Other: ______________________________

Reminder: Tax rules are technical and can change. This planner helps you stay organized and funded. Your tax professional applies the correct tax treatment for your situation.

1099s & Barter for Freelancers & Independent Contractors

What you might get... and what it does not mean

Freelancers and independent contractors panic every January for one reason: forms show up that don't match deposits, and deposits show up with no forms at all.

Here's the reality:

You can get paid and receive no 1099

A 1099 is not a "permission slip" for income. It's an information form.
If you earn it, it's still income—even if no form arrives.

You can receive a 1099 that doesn't match your bank deposits

Common reasons:

- **processing fees removed before deposit (Stripe/PayPal/Square/etc.)**
- **refunds or chargebacks happened later**
- **payouts were delayed into a different month (timing differences)**
- **multiple payments were batched into one deposit**
- **a deposit was split across multiple deposits**
- **reserve holds or withheld amounts**
- **you changed payout accounts mid-year**

The common 1099 forms you may see

(Forms and reporting rules can change—confirm current-year rules.)

- **1099-NEC: often used when a client pays you as a nonemployee contractor**
- **1099-K: often tied to third-party payment processing (card payments and some payment platforms), depending on current rules**
- **1099-MISC: sometimes used for certain payment types that aren't nonemployee compensation (less common for standard freelance client work, but possible)**

Bartering isn't "free" income — it's still taxable.

If you receive goods or services in exchange for your work (for example, a photographer trades you a shoot for promotion, a brand trades product for content, or you swap editing for web design), the IRS generally treats the fair market value of what you received as business income, even if no cash changed hands.

Record the date, who you traded with, what you provided, what you received, and a reasonable value for both sides (screenshots, price lists, invoices, or marketplace comps help).

Also record any related expenses you paid out of pocket to complete the barter.

Good barter records protect you two ways: they support the income that should be reported, and they preserve the deductions tied to earning it.

The only "winning" approach

Instead of chasing forms, track and reconcile:

1. **Income records (invoices/receipts/earnings summaries)**
2. **Fees/adjustments (processor fees, platform fees, instant payout fees)**
3. **Refunds/chargebacks (if applicable)**
4. **Net deposits (what hit your bank)**

That's why this book includes the reconciliation pages.

Reminder: If the numbers don't line up, don't guess. Use your reports and reconciliation pages and ask your tax pro if something looks off.

NON-CASH COMPENSATION / BARTER LOG (OPTIONAL)

Use this page only if you are paid with something other than cash.

Most freelancers and independent contractors get paid in dollars. But sometimes you're compensated with products, equipment, services, credits, free access, travel, or "trade" work instead of (or in addition to) a normal payment.

This page exists for one reason: so, you don't forget what you received and why you received it.

What counts as non-cash compensation (freelancer examples)

You may want to log items like:

- **products or equipment provided as part of a client agreement**
- **free or discounted services received in exchange for your work (barter)**
- **credits, gift cards, account credits, or fee waivers used for business purposes**
- **paid travel or lodging tied to a job**
- **a subscription or software license provided "in exchange for services"**

Yes—this includes "free stuff"

If a client sends you something as compensation, it's still part of the business transaction.
Don't guess. Don't ignore it. Just track it. Your tax professional will apply the correct treatment.

One simple rule that keeps this clean

If you would be embarrassed to explain why you received it, it belongs on this page.

WORKSHEET: NON-CASH COMPENSATION / BARTER LOG (OPTIONAL)

(Record what you received, when you received it, the business purpose, and any value information available.)

Date	Particulars	Purpose	Value	Notes

Reminder: Rules can be technical and may change. This log does not determine tax treatment—it prevents missing facts.

WORKSHEET: 1099 Tracker + Mismatch Notes 1099 TRACKER + MISMATCH NOTES

Tax Year: __________ Freelancer Brand: ________________________

Payer / Platform	Form Type (NEC/K/Other)	Amount on Form	Amount Deposited (if known)	Difference	Why it differed (fees, refunds, etc.)	Notes / Proof Saved

INTERNATIONAL CLIENT INCOME

Foreign clients, currency conversion, and "why is there withholding?"

If you collaborate with clients outside the U.S. or get paid in foreign currency, your bookkeeping needs one extra layer:

Convert consistently, document clearly, and keep the proof.

What Changes With International Income

When you're paid internationally, you may see:

- **payment received in a foreign currency**
- **currency conversion fees**
- **withholding taken out before you receive funds**
- **deposits that change depending on exchange-rate timing**
- **foreign statements or forms (or no forms at all)**

None of this is unusual. It just needs clean records.

The Best Habit

For each international payment, log:

- **date paid**
- **client/platform name**
- **original currency amount (if available)**
- **amount received in U.S. dollars (USD)**
- **exchange rate / conversion notes (how you converted)**
- **fees and withholding**
- **proof saved (statement, payout report, screenshot)**

Reminder: International tax issues can get technical fast. This log doesn't replace advice—it prevents missing facts.

WORKSHEET: INTERNATIONAL PAYMENT LOG

Tax Year: __________ Freelancer Brand: ______________________

Date Paid	Brand / Platform	Currency	Amount (foreign)	USD Received	Fees / Witholding	Conversion Method / Notes	Proof Saved

YEAR-END WRAP-UP CHECKLIST

(Use this to close your books cleanly before tax filing.)

1) Income & Deposits: make the money trail make sense

✓ Save year-end income records (invoice list, client payment summaries, any 1099s received)
✓ Save year-end payment processor reports (Stripe/PayPal/Square/etc.) if used
✓ Reconcile income so it's explainable: gross paid/earned → fees/refunds/chargebacks → net deposits
✓ Reconcile bank and credit card statements (business accounts + any mixed-use cards you deduct from)

2) Expenses & Receipts: don't lose deductions you already paid for

✓ Confirm receipts are saved and expenses are categorized
✓ Add a business-purpose note for anything that could look personal ("Amazon," "Target," "Best Buy," "Misc.")
✓ Review common freelancer "leak" areas:

- **processing/banking fees**
- **subscriptions/software renewals**
- **small recurring tools/apps**
- **professional services (bookkeeping, legal, tax prep)**
- **travel/parking/tolls for client work**
  ✓ Confirm your totals are accurate (income totals and expense totals by category)

3) Client projects: track job costs, reimbursables, and profitability

✓ Review Client Project Costs & Reimbursables pages: make sure job-related costs are logged
✓ Confirm reimbursables were either (a) billed to clients or (b) intentionally absorbed
✓ Optional (smart): complete Project Profit Snapshots for major projects/retainerships

4) Contractors, subcontractors, and employees: paperwork that sneaks up fast

✓ Compile contract labor records (who you paid, what for, how much, when)
✓ Confirm you have W-9s (or W-8 forms where applicable) on file when needed
✓ Issue 1099 forms by January 31 if required

- Note: rules and thresholds can change—confirm current-year requirements.
  ✓ If you have employees: handle payroll through a payroll service and generate W-2/W-3 forms as required (employees only)

5) Home office, mileage, and mixed-use items

✓ Verify Home Office Worksheet(s) are completed

- Use Office Space #2 if you moved or changed your primary workspace during the year
  ✓ Update mileage totals and make sure entries include a business purpose note
  ✓ Review mixed-use percentages (phone/internet/vehicle/home office) and document changes
  ✓ Verify self-employed health insurance tracking is complete (if applicable)

6) Assets & equipment: don't forget the big stuff

✓ Update your Equipment & Asset Log (computers, phones, printers, specialized tools, office equipment, etc.)
✓ Complete "Assets to Review With Your Tax Pro" for major purchases
✓ Document any item sold, traded, disposed of, lost, or stolen (date + amount received/credit + notes)

7) Physical products / inventory (only if applicable)

✓ If you sell physical products: compile COGS info (inventory counts, product/material costs, shipping/packaging, fulfillment fees)

8) Digital products (only if applicable)

✓ If you sell digital products: summarize gross sales, platform/processing fees, refunds/chargebacks, and contractor costs

9) Retirement contributions and funding deadlines (if applicable)

✓ Confirm retirement plan contributions and deadlines (especially if you fund after year-end)

10) Prepare the clean tax package

✓ Create one organized folder set for tax filing:

- **income records + any 1099s received**
- **processor summaries + deposit reconciliation pages**
- **expense totals + supporting receipts**
- **client project costs/reimbursables + profit snapshots (if used)**
- **contractor totals + W-9/W-8 status**
- **assets/equipment logs + changes**
- **home office + mileage + health insurance worksheets**

✓ Write down any "odd items" for your tax pro:

- **large refunds/chargebacks**
- **unusual deposits or mismatches**
- **international client payments**
- **major travel**
- **major equipment purchases**
- **major subcontractor costs tied to specific projects**

More Tools for Entrepreneurs:

MONEY WITH AMY SERIES
Smart Money Moves:
Mastering Replacement,
Irregular Expense,
and
Property Ownership Budgets
Exclusive Reader Gift - Details Inside
Amy Rose Herrick
Profit-Building Specialist
International Best Selling Author
Free Audio Version Included

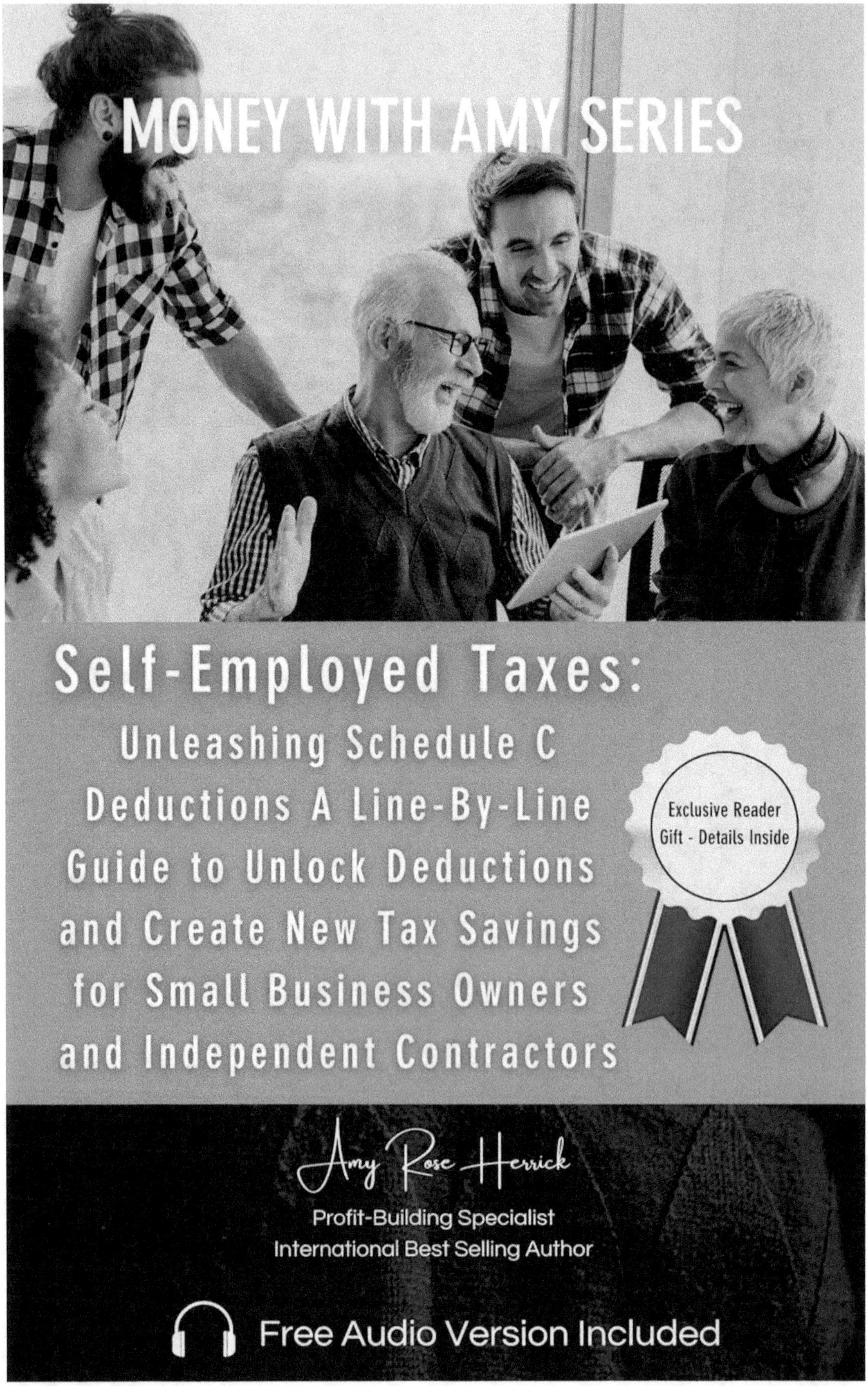
MONEY WITH AMY SERIES
Self-Employed Taxes:
Unleashing Schedule C Deductions A Line-By-Line Guide to Unlock Deductions and Create New Tax Savings for Small Business Owners and Independent Contractors
Exclusive Reader Gift - Details Inside
Amy Rose Herrick
Profit-Building Specialist
International Best Selling Author
Free Audio Version Included

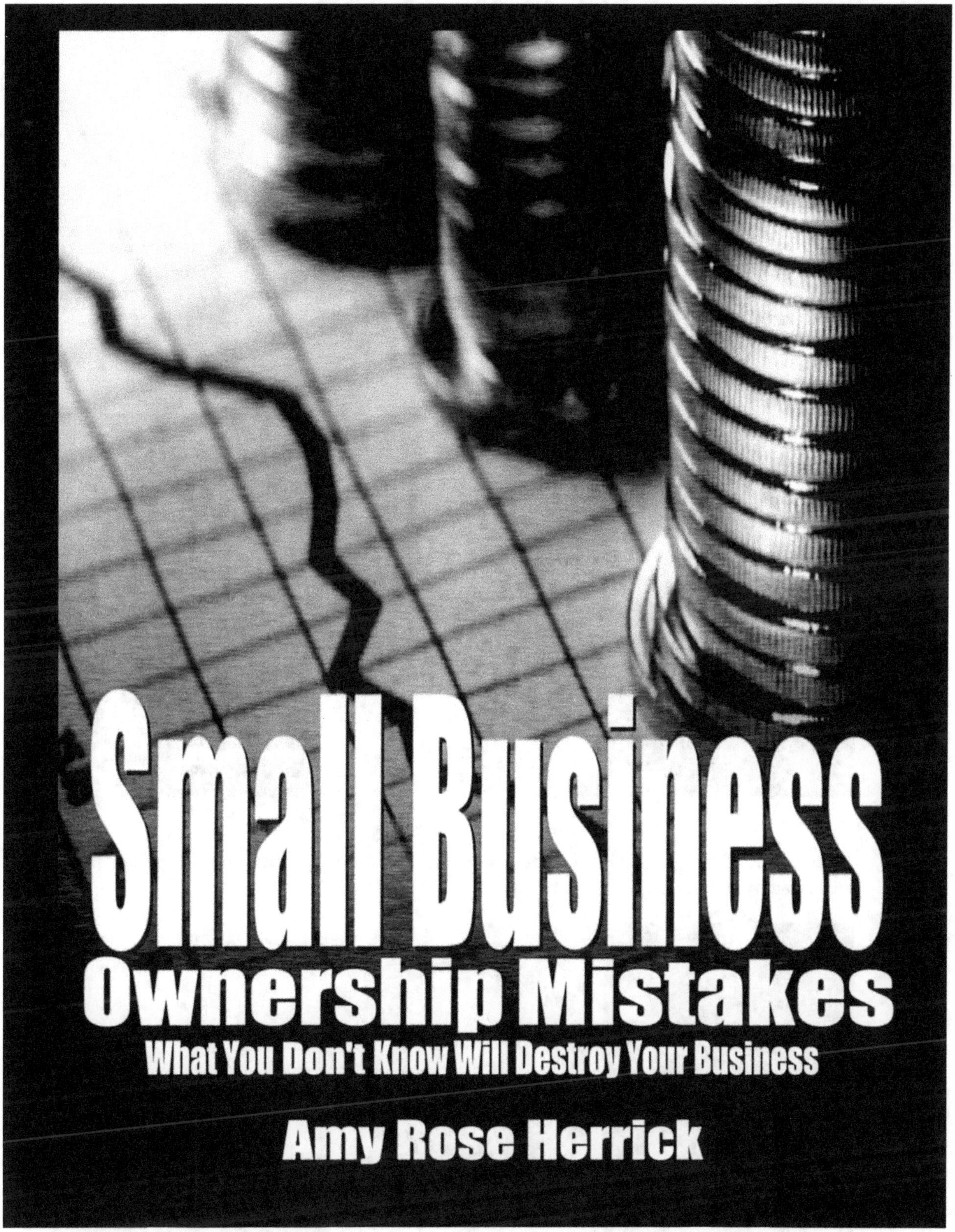
Small Business
Ownership Mistakes
What You Don't Know Will Destroy Your Business
Amy Rose Herrick

Mileage Log Book Referral (Optional)

Vehicle mileage must be tracked separately.

Any mileage log used should meet IRS recordkeeping requirements.

Please refer to your dedicated Mileage Log Book for all mileage-related deductions.

Deluxe version Mileage Log Book Titles on Amazon for consideration with IRS compliance helps with separate sections for business, medical, charitable and volunteer mileage included authored by A. Herrick:

Basic version Mileage Log Book Titles on Amazon with only business mileage logs included authored by A. Herrick:

www.ingramcontent.com/pod-product-compliance
Lightning Source LLC
LaVergne TN
LVHW080044210926
848481LV00011B/3280
* 9 7 8 1 9 6 0 4 2 7 5 8 8 *